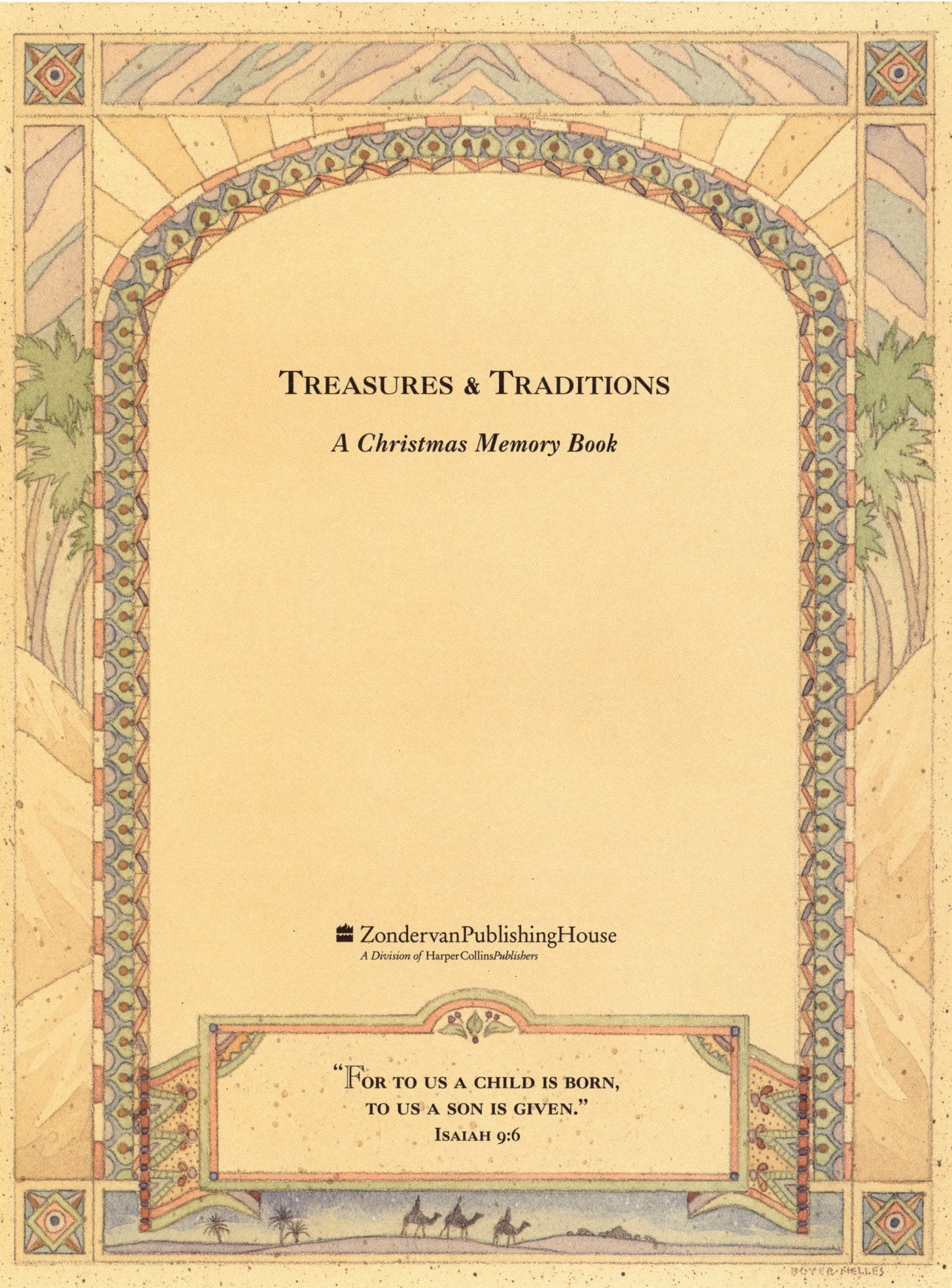

Treasures & Traditions

A Christmas Memory Book

ZondervanPublishingHouse
A Division of HarperCollinsPublishers

"For to us a child is born,
to us a son is given."
Isaiah 9:6

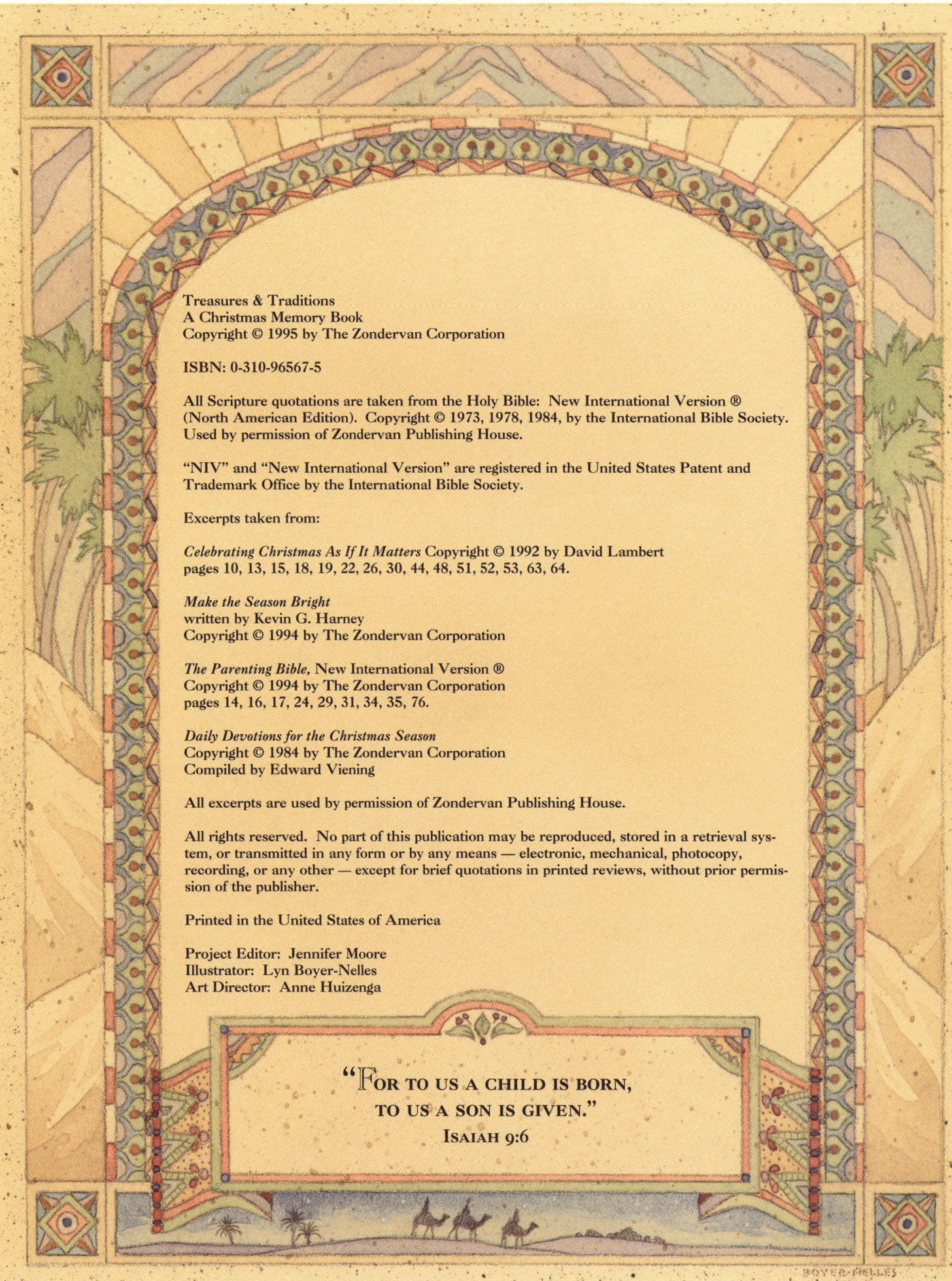

Treasures & Traditions
A Christmas Memory Book
Copyright © 1995 by The Zondervan Corporation

ISBN: 0-310-96567-5

All Scripture quotations are taken from the Holy Bible: New International Version ® (North American Edition). Copyright © 1973, 1978, 1984, by the International Bible Society. Used by permission of Zondervan Publishing House.

"NIV" and "New International Version" are registered in the United States Patent and Trademark Office by the International Bible Society.

Excerpts taken from:

Celebrating Christmas As If It Matters Copyright © 1992 by David Lambert
pages 10, 13, 15, 18, 19, 22, 26, 30, 44, 48, 51, 52, 53, 63, 64.

Make the Season Bright
written by Kevin G. Harney
Copyright © 1994 by The Zondervan Corporation

The Parenting Bible, New International Version ®
Copyright © 1994 by The Zondervan Corporation
pages 14, 16, 17, 24, 29, 31, 34, 35, 76.

Daily Devotions for the Christmas Season
Copyright © 1984 by The Zondervan Corporation
Compiled by Edward Viening

All excerpts are used by permission of Zondervan Publishing House.

All rights reserved. No part of this publication may be reproduced, stored in a retrieval system, or transmitted in any form or by any means — electronic, mechanical, photocopy, recording, or any other — except for brief quotations in printed reviews, without prior permission of the publisher.

Printed in the United States of America

Project Editor: Jennifer Moore
Illustrator: Lyn Boyer-Nelles
Art Director: Anne Huizenga

"FOR TO US A CHILD IS BORN,
TO US A SON IS GIVEN."
ISAIAH 9:6

Glory to the newborn King

"For to us a child is born, to us a son is given."
Isaiah 9:6

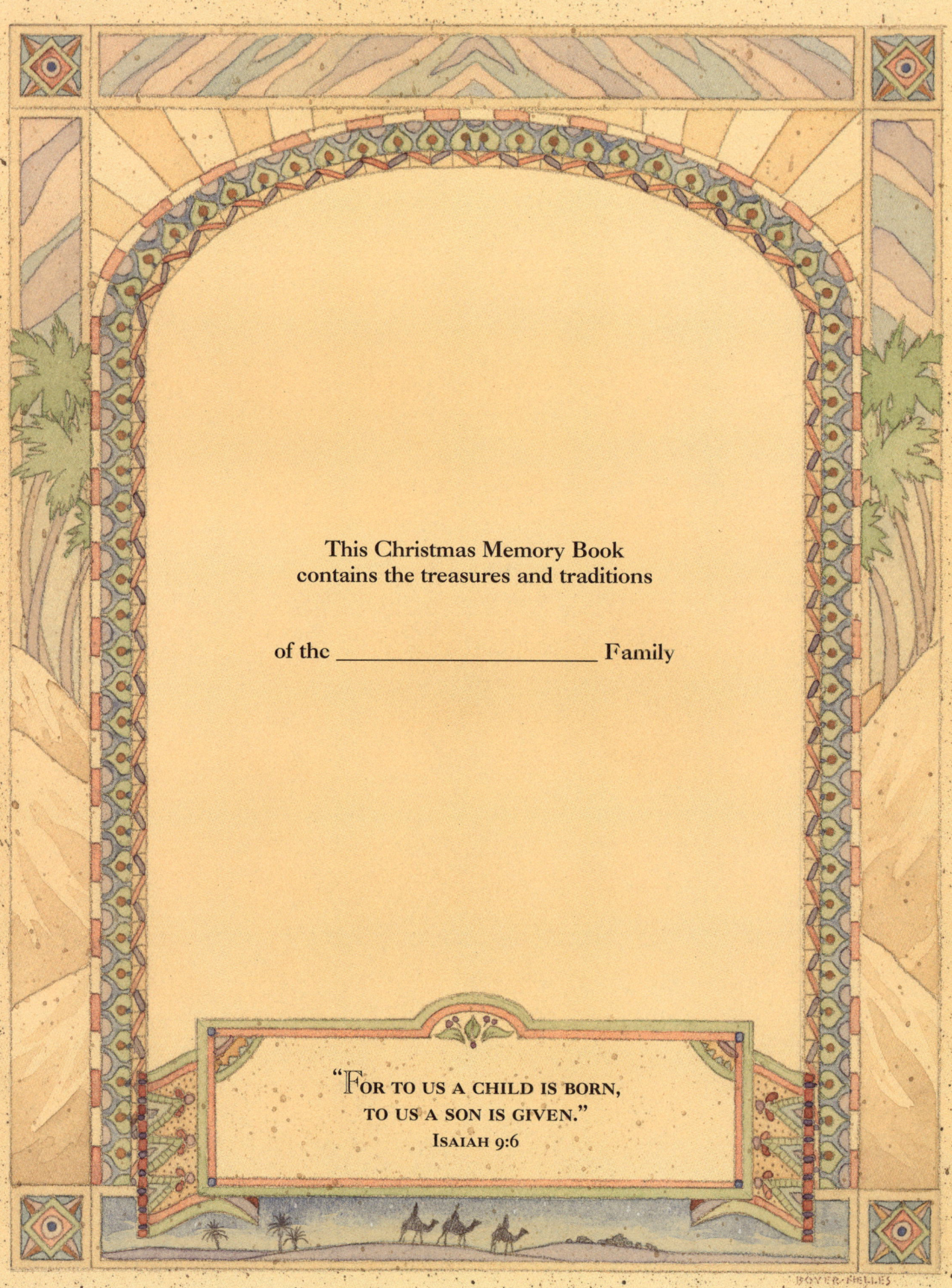

This Christmas Memory Book
contains the treasures and traditions

of the _____ Family

"For to us a child is born,
to us a son is given."
Isaiah 9:6

Table of Contents

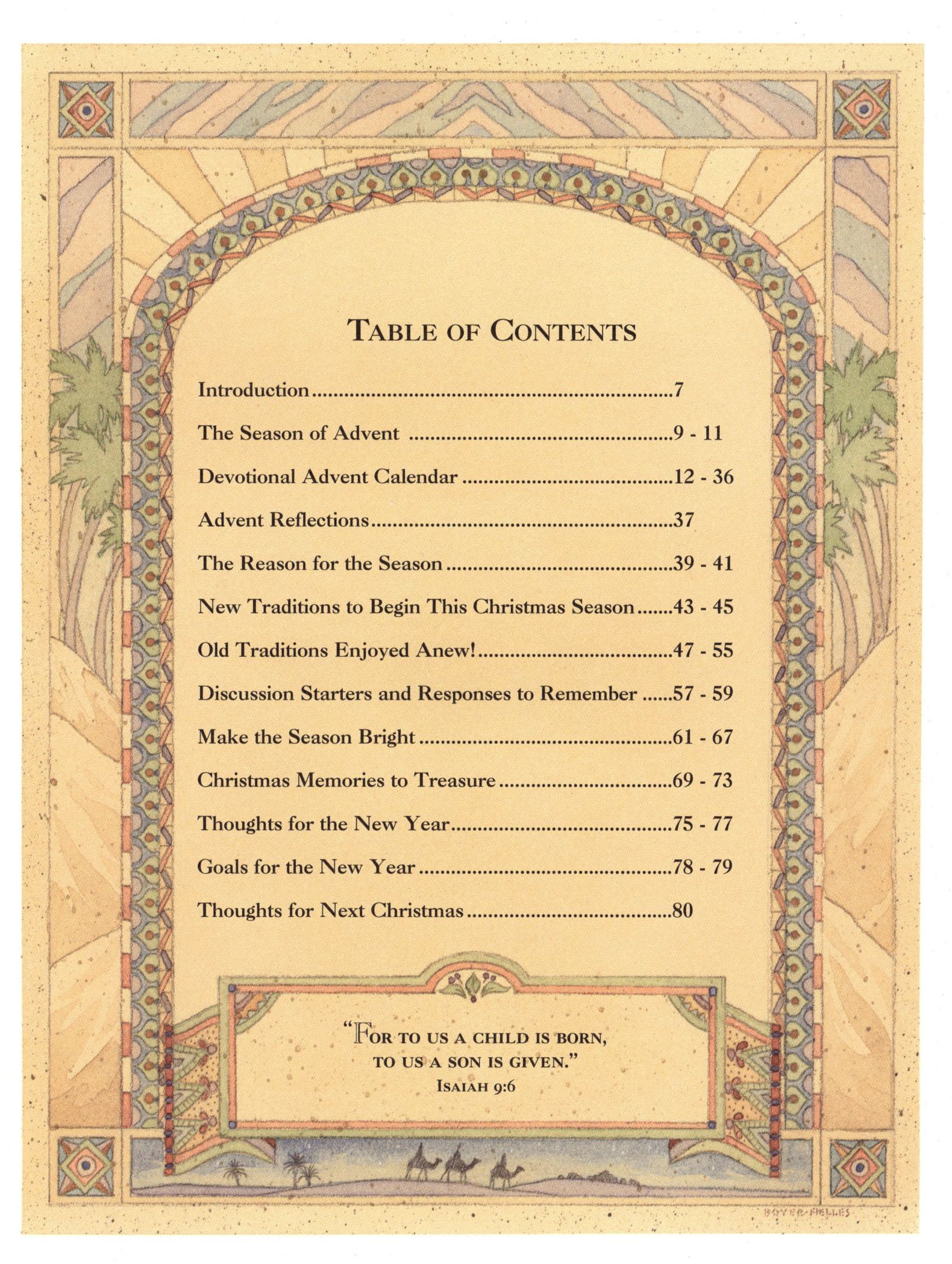

Introduction 7

The Season of Advent .... 9 - 11

Devotional Advent Calendar .... 12 - 36

Advent Reflections 37

The Reason for the Season .... 39 - 41

New Traditions to Begin This Christmas Season ...... 43 - 45

Old Traditions Enjoyed Anew! .... 47 - 55

Discussion Starters and Responses to Remember ...... 57 - 59

Make the Season Bright .... 61 - 67

Christmas Memories to Treasure .... 69 - 73

Thoughts for the New Year .... 75 - 77

Goals for the New Year .... 78 - 79

Thoughts for Next Christmas 80

"For to us a child is born,
to us a son is given."
Isaiah 9:6

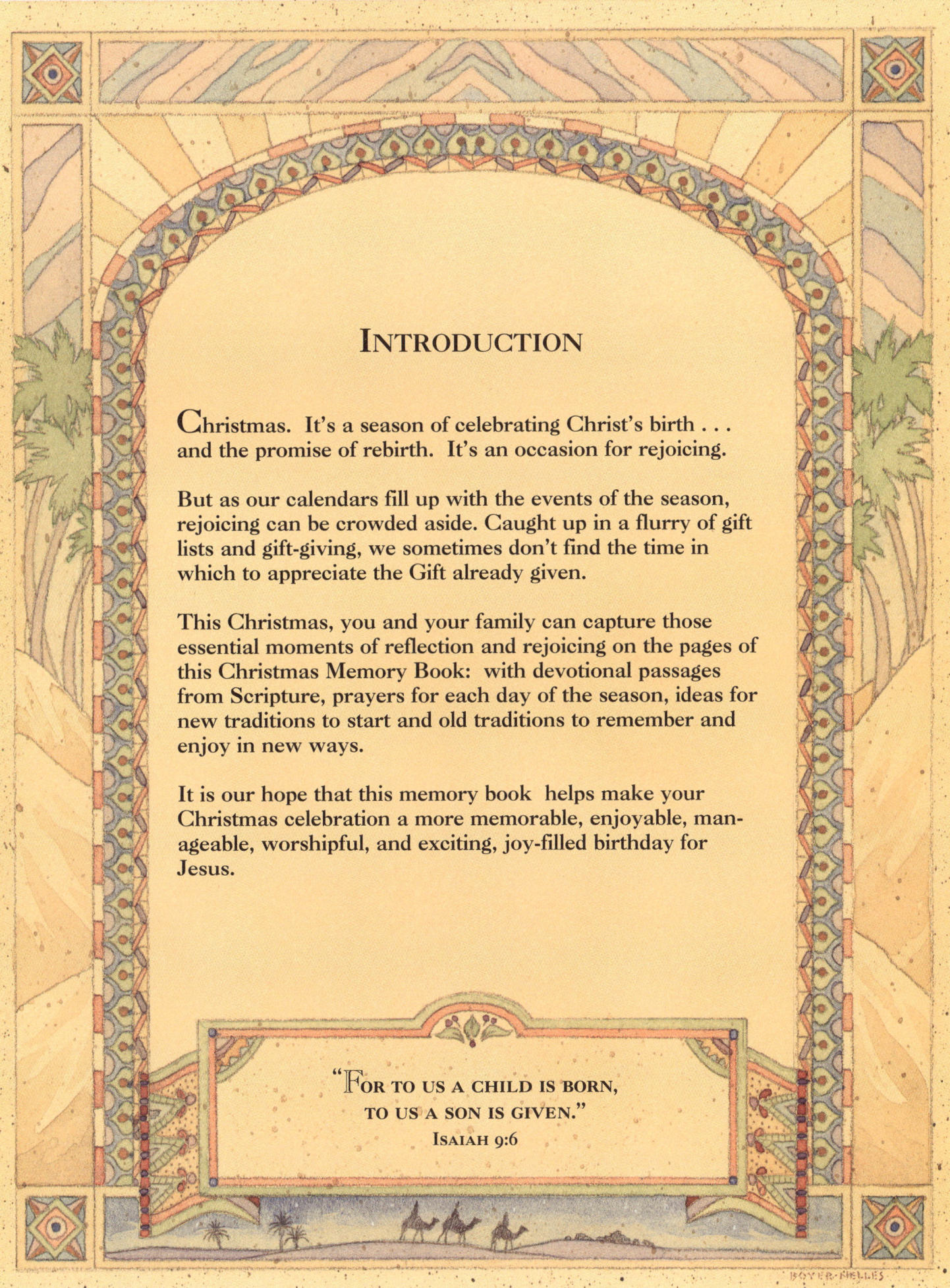

INTRODUCTION

Christmas. It's a season of celebrating Christ's birth . . . and the promise of rebirth. It's an occasion for rejoicing.

But as our calendars fill up with the events of the season, rejoicing can be crowded aside. Caught up in a flurry of gift lists and gift-giving, we sometimes don't find the time in which to appreciate the Gift already given.

This Christmas, you and your family can capture those essential moments of reflection and rejoicing on the pages of this Christmas Memory Book: with devotional passages from Scripture, prayers for each day of the season, ideas for new traditions to start and old traditions to remember and enjoy in new ways.

It is our hope that this memory book helps make your Christmas celebration a more memorable, enjoyable, manageable, worshipful, and exciting, joy-filled birthday for Jesus.

"For to us a child is born,
to us a son is given."
Isaiah 9:6

The Season of Advent

"I bring you good news of great joy that will be for all the people."
Luke 2:10

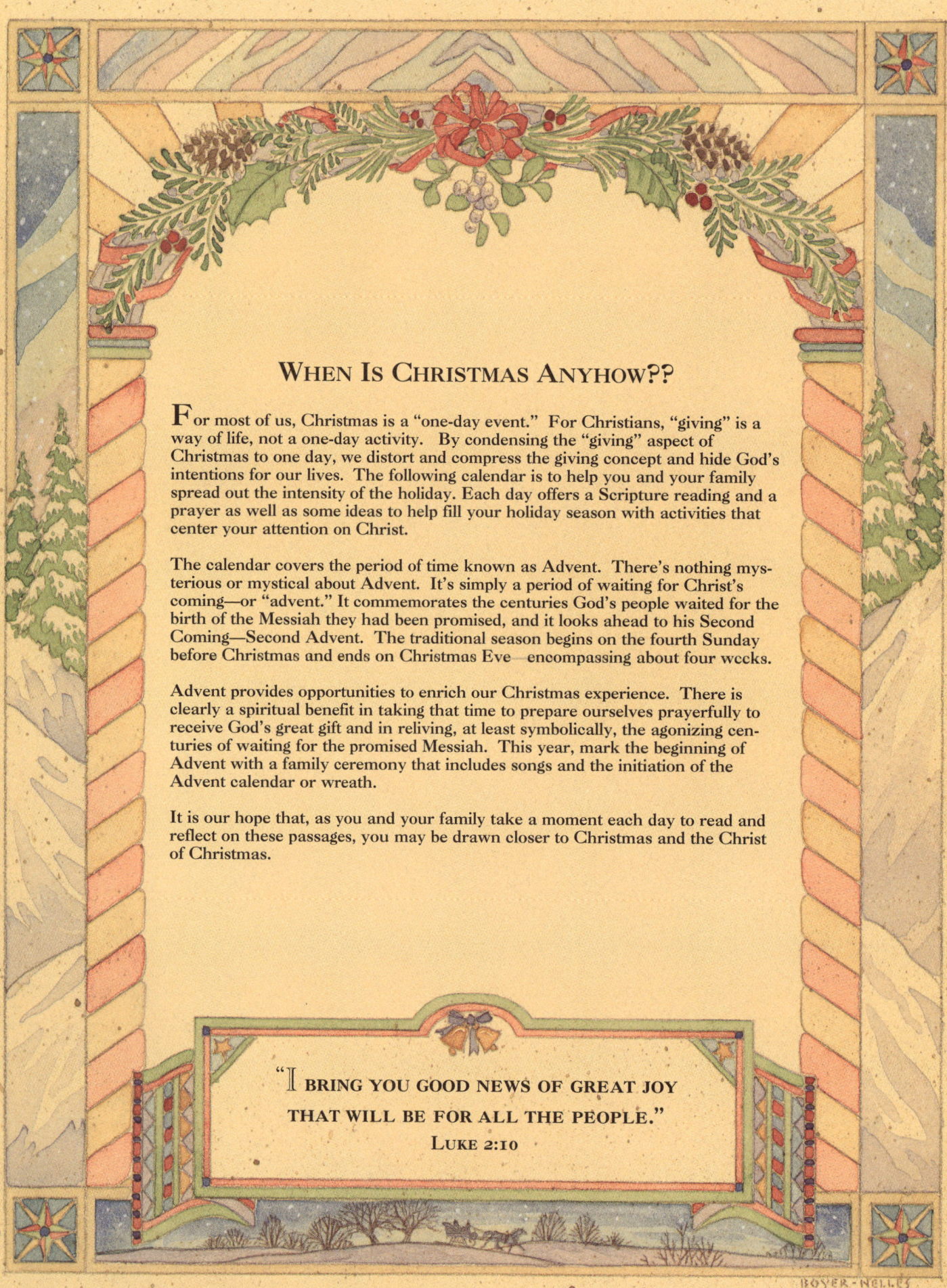

When Is Christmas Anyhow??

For most of us, Christmas is a "one-day event." For Christians, "giving" is a way of life, not a one-day activity. By condensing the "giving" aspect of Christmas to one day, we distort and compress the giving concept and hide God's intentions for our lives. The following calendar is to help you and your family spread out the intensity of the holiday. Each day offers a Scripture reading and a prayer as well as some ideas to help fill your holiday season with activities that center your attention on Christ.

The calendar covers the period of time known as Advent. There's nothing mysterious or mystical about Advent. It's simply a period of waiting for Christ's coming—or "advent." It commemorates the centuries God's people waited for the birth of the Messiah they had been promised, and it looks ahead to his Second Coming—Second Advent. The traditional season begins on the fourth Sunday before Christmas and ends on Christmas Eve—encompassing about four weeks.

Advent provides opportunities to enrich our Christmas experience. There is clearly a spiritual benefit in taking that time to prepare ourselves prayerfully to receive God's great gift and in reliving, at least symbolically, the agonizing centuries of waiting for the promised Messiah. This year, mark the beginning of Advent with a family ceremony that includes songs and the initiation of the Advent calendar or wreath.

It is our hope that, as you and your family take a moment each day to read and reflect on these passages, you may be drawn closer to Christmas and the Christ of Christmas.

"I BRING YOU GOOD NEWS OF GREAT JOY
THAT WILL BE FOR ALL THE PEOPLE."
LUKE 2:10

Our Family Advent Ceremony

Record your family's Advent Ceremony below. Celebrate the start of this joyous season with song, prayer, and reflection.

Songs

Prayers

Reflections

"I BRING YOU GOOD NEWS OF GREAT JOY
THAT WILL BE FOR ALL THE PEOPLE."
LUKE 2:10

December 1

But when the time had fully come, God sent his Son, born of a woman, born under law, to redeem those under law, that we might receive the full rights of sons. Because you are sons, God sent the Spirit of his Son into our hearts, the Spirit who calls out, "ABBA, Father." So you are no longer a slave, but a son; and since you are a son, God has made you also an heir.
Galatians 4:4-7

We thank you today, our Father, for the promise you made to your first children that in due time you would send your Son to crush the serpent and redeem your people from their sins. We rejoice that when the time was come, our Lord was born to give himself as a ransom for many. We ask that you will make this Christmas season a time of spiritual refreshment and praise. In Jesus' name. Amen.

Christ is Christmas

Plan a special gift or act of giving for someone for each day of this Advent Season. Try anonymous gifts, prayers, or letters to someone special. Reveal the source of these acts of kindness on Christmas day.

"I BRING YOU GOOD NEWS OF GREAT JOY THAT WILL BE FOR ALL THE PEOPLE."
LUKE 2:10

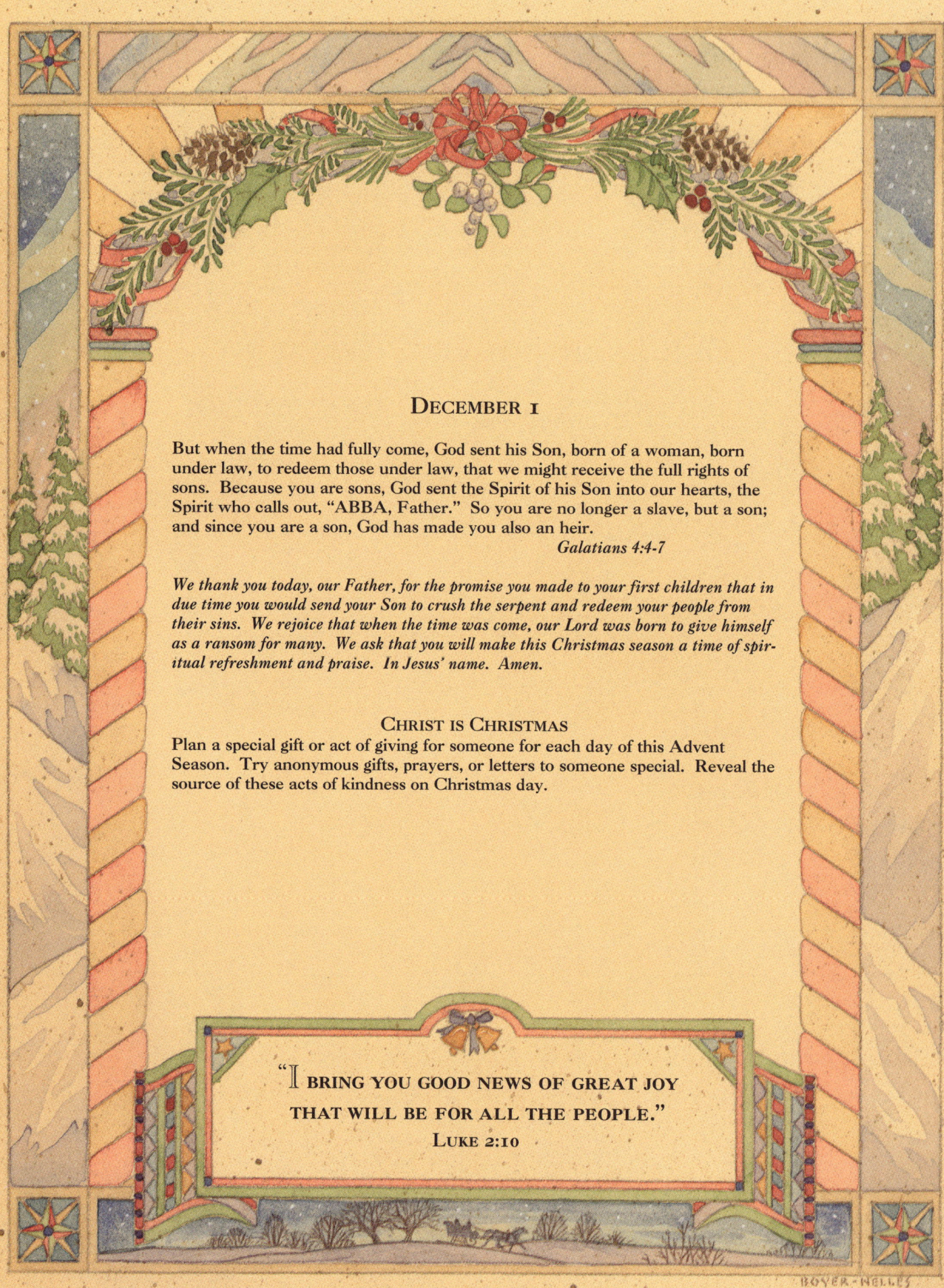

December 2

Therefore the Lord himself will give you a sign: The virgin will be with child and will give birth to a son, and will call him Immanuel.

Isaiah 7:14

We are reminded again, our Father, that "nothing is impossible with God." One of the thrills of the Christmas season is the realization that our Lord's birth was a miracle—he was born of a virgin. May this truth cause us to praise your name anew for your great love with which you loved us, through Jesus Christ our Lord. Amen.

Christ is Christmas

Create a Waiting Tree—a tree decorated with symbols of waiting—an acorn, an egg, a cocoon, a sunrise, a seed, a tadpole, and so on. You can use your Christmas tree, mount a tree branch, or even create a tree out of construction paper or felt to hang on the wall.

"I BRING YOU GOOD NEWS OF GREAT JOY THAT WILL BE FOR ALL THE PEOPLE."
LUKE 2:10

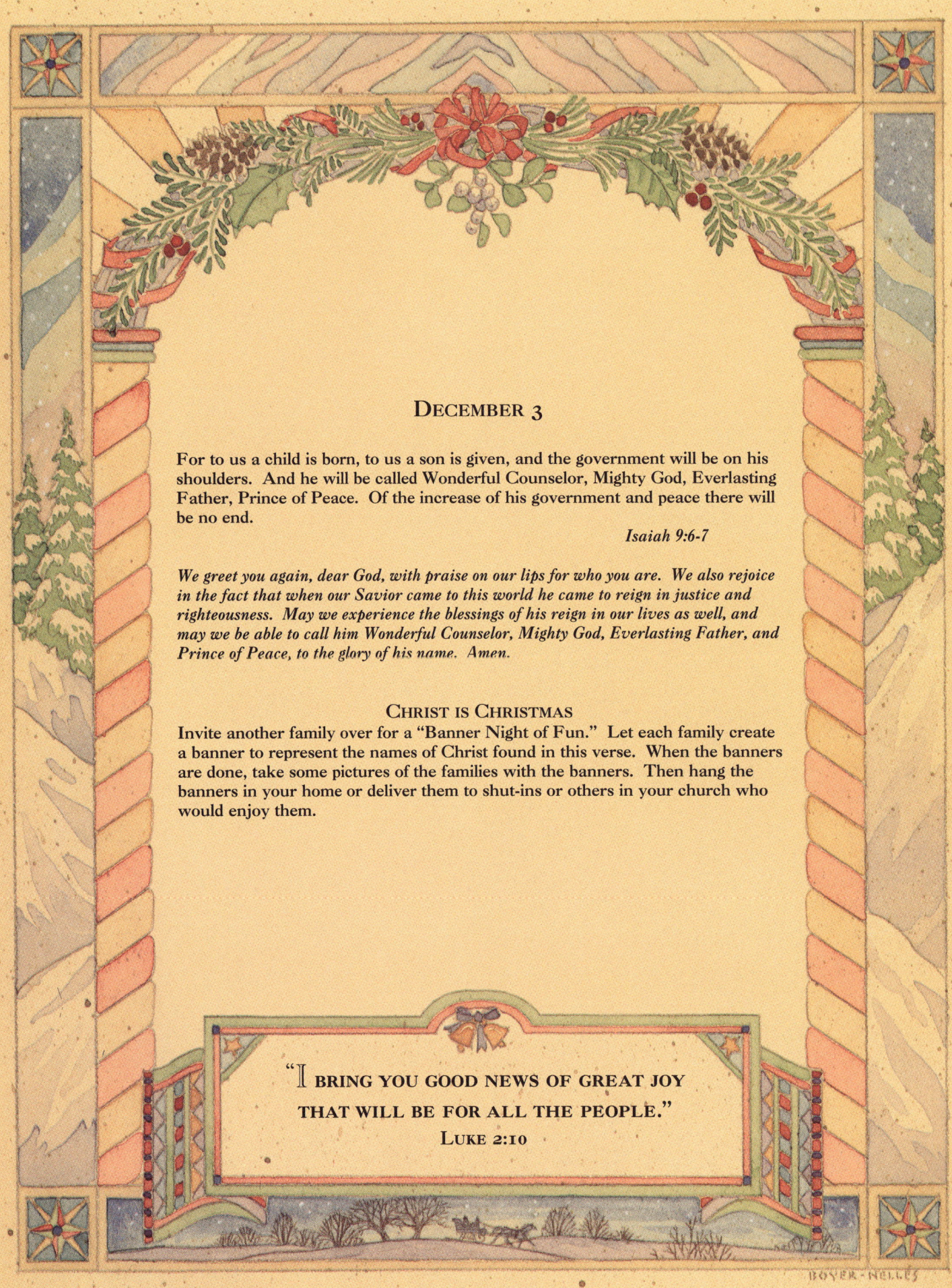

December 3

For to us a child is born, to us a son is given, and the government will be on his shoulders. And he will be called Wonderful Counselor, Mighty God, Everlasting Father, Prince of Peace. Of the increase of his government and peace there will be no end.

Isaiah 9:6-7

We greet you again, dear God, with praise on our lips for who you are. We also rejoice in the fact that when our Savior came to this world he came to reign in justice and righteousness. May we experience the blessings of his reign in our lives as well, and may we be able to call him Wonderful Counselor, Mighty God, Everlasting Father, and Prince of Peace, to the glory of his name. Amen.

Christ is Christmas

Invite another family over for a "Banner Night of Fun." Let each family create a banner to represent the names of Christ found in this verse. When the banners are done, take some pictures of the families with the banners. Then hang the banners in your home or deliver them to shut-ins or others in your church who would enjoy them.

> "I bring you good news of great joy that will be for all the people."
> Luke 2:10

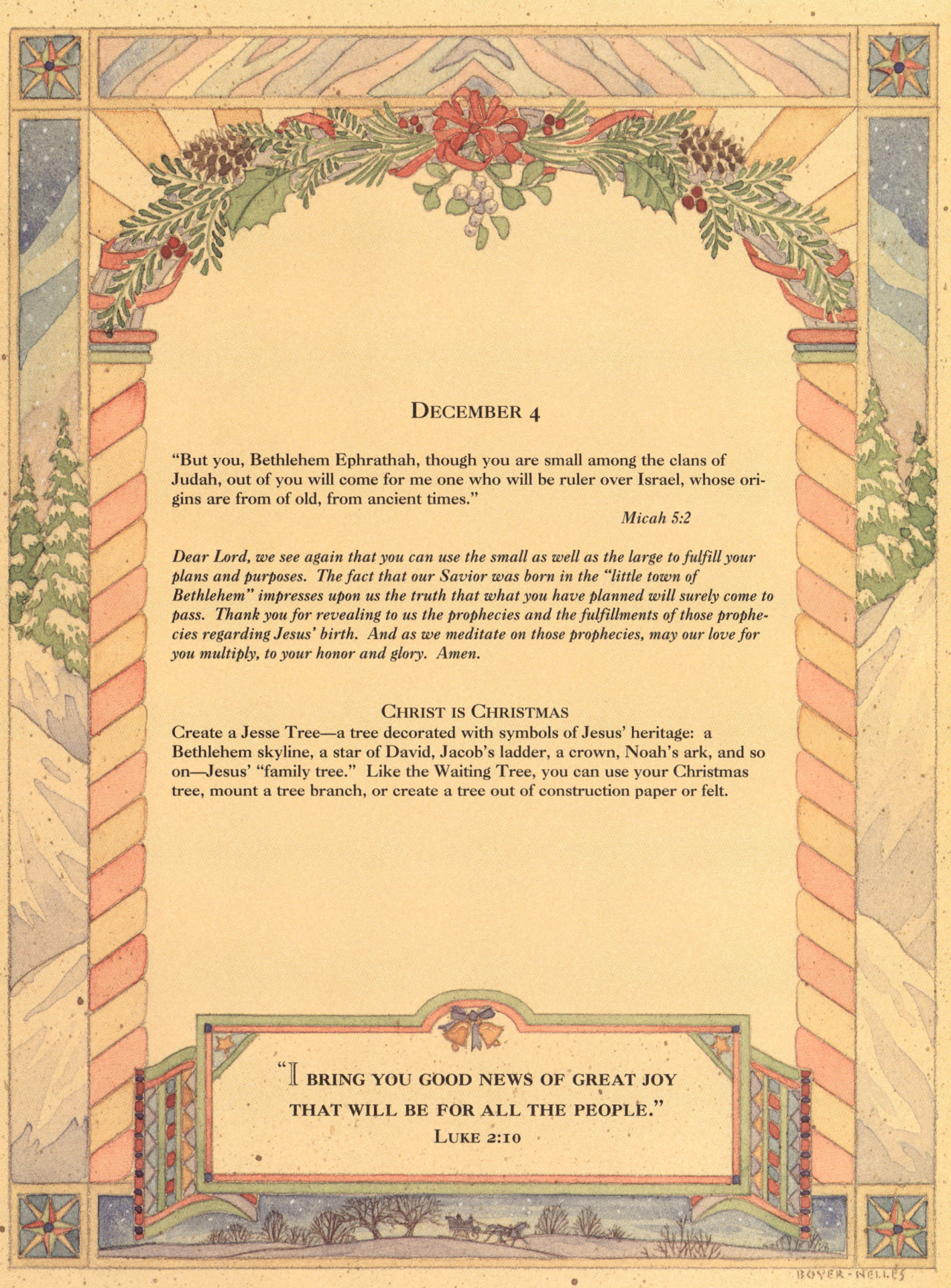

December 4

"But you, Bethlehem Ephrathah, though you are small among the clans of Judah, out of you will come for me one who will be ruler over Israel, whose origins are from of old, from ancient times."

Micah 5:2

Dear Lord, we see again that you can use the small as well as the large to fulfill your plans and purposes. The fact that our Savior was born in the "little town of Bethlehem" impresses upon us the truth that what you have planned will surely come to pass. Thank you for revealing to us the prophecies and the fulfillments of those prophecies regarding Jesus' birth. And as we meditate on those prophecies, may our love for you multiply, to your honor and glory. Amen.

Christ is Christmas

Create a Jesse Tree—a tree decorated with symbols of Jesus' heritage: a Bethlehem skyline, a star of David, Jacob's ladder, a crown, Noah's ark, and so on—Jesus' "family tree." Like the Waiting Tree, you can use your Christmas tree, mount a tree branch, or create a tree out of construction paper or felt.

"I BRING YOU GOOD NEWS OF GREAT JOY THAT WILL BE FOR ALL THE PEOPLE."
LUKE 2:10

December 5

Mary was greatly troubled at his words and wondered what kind of greeting this might be. But the angel said to her, "Do not be afraid, Mary, you have found favor with God. You will be with child and give birth to a son, and you are to give him the name Jesus."

Luke 1:29-31

Heavenly Father, as the angel announced to Mary the forthcoming birth of our Lord, so may we announce to those around us that Jesus Christ was born the Savior of the world. We may not understand how all of this came about but we do know that Jesus came for us, and that if we receive him into our hearts, we have eternal life. Help us to share this blessed truth with others, for Jesus' sake. Amen.

Christ is Christmas

Involve your family in a secret giving project. From your community or church, choose a family in difficult financial circumstances. Swear everyone in your family to secrecy and provide the needy family with a special surprise each of the four weeks before Christmas. One week provide all the food for a special meal. The next week wrap up gloves or hats for each person in the family. Another week send concert or movie tickets. Be creative. Your kids will learn a valuable lesson, and the family will "overflow" with thanks to God.

"I BRING YOU GOOD NEWS OF GREAT JOY
THAT WILL BE FOR ALL THE PEOPLE."
LUKE 2:10

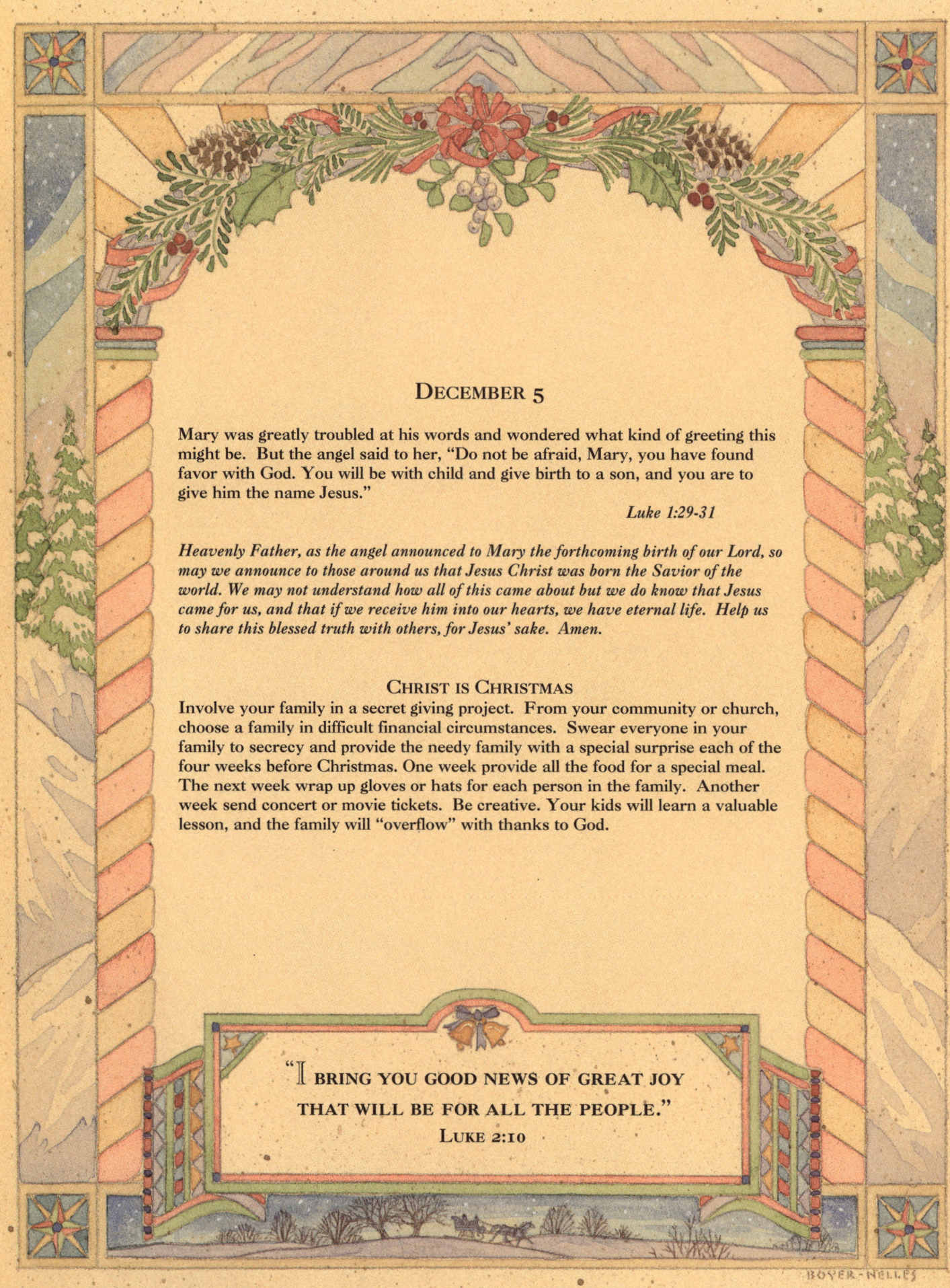

December 6

Because Joseph [Mary's husband] was a righteous man and did not want to expose her to public disgrace, he had in mind to divorce her quietly. But after he had considered this, an angel of the Lord appeared to him in a dream and said, "Joseph, son of David, do not be afraid to take Mary home as your wife, because what is conceived in her is from the Holy Spirit. She will give birth to a son, and you are to give him the name Jesus, because he will save people from their sins.
Matthew 1:19-21

Our Father in heaven, our hearts are filled with gratitude today when we realize it was our sins that caused the Lord to leave the "ivory palaces" above and come to this sinful world. The announcement that the angel made to Joseph, that Jesus would "save his people from their sins," brought hope to a troubled world, and it brings hope to us today. We acknowledge that we sin against you, and we confess those sins today. "Thank you, Lord, for making us whole," through Jesus Christ our Lord, in whose name we pray. Amen.

Christ is Christmas

In recognition of the reason for Christ's birth, let each family member confess a sin and seek forgiveness. Then make homemade ornaments from construction paper. On one side write "I confess" and on the other side, "You're forgiven." Decorate with sparkling glitter and hang these ornaments on the tree as reminders that we can confess and be sure God will forgive us of all of our sins.

"I bring you good news of great joy that will be for all the people."
Luke 2:10

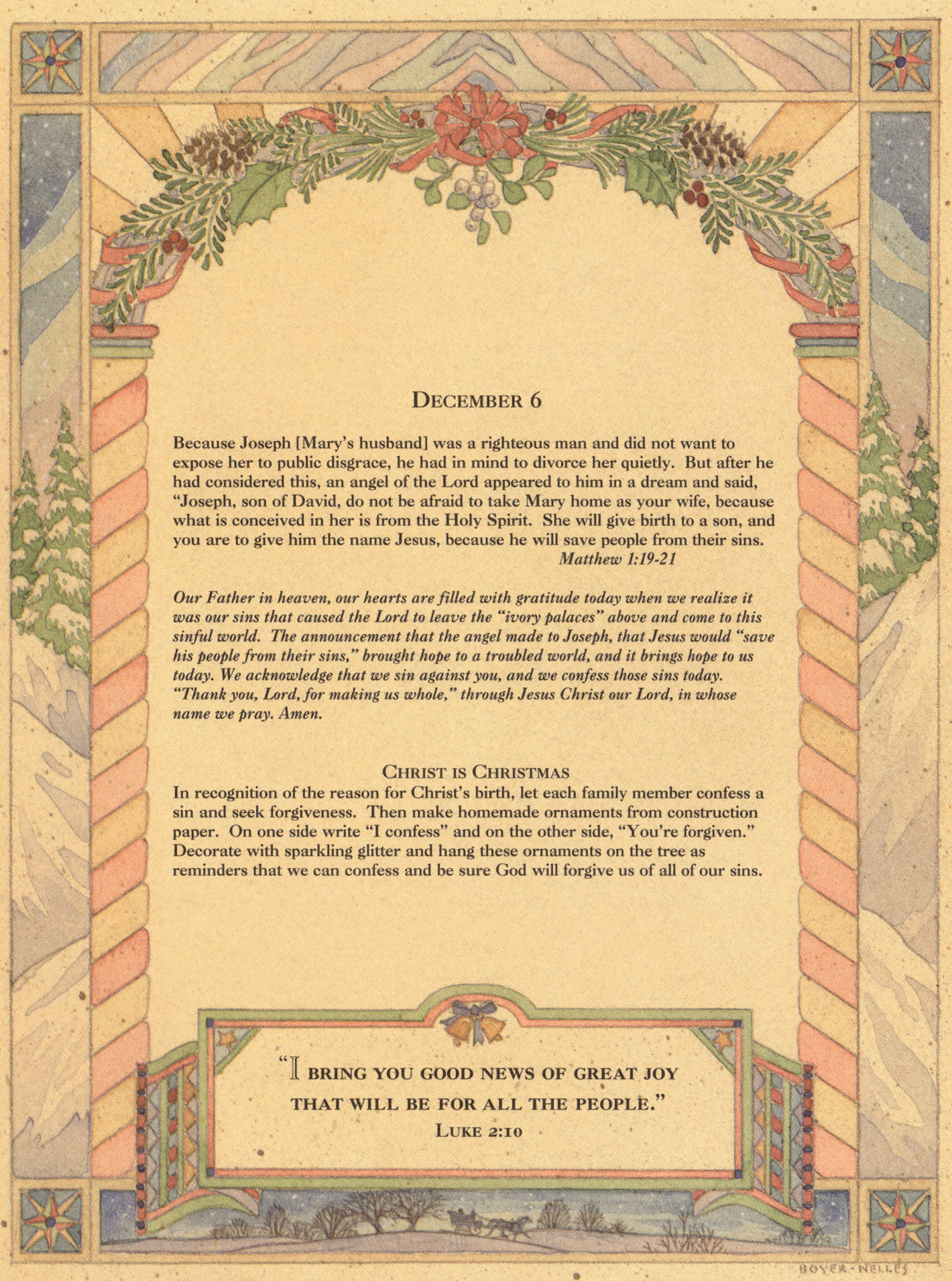

December 7

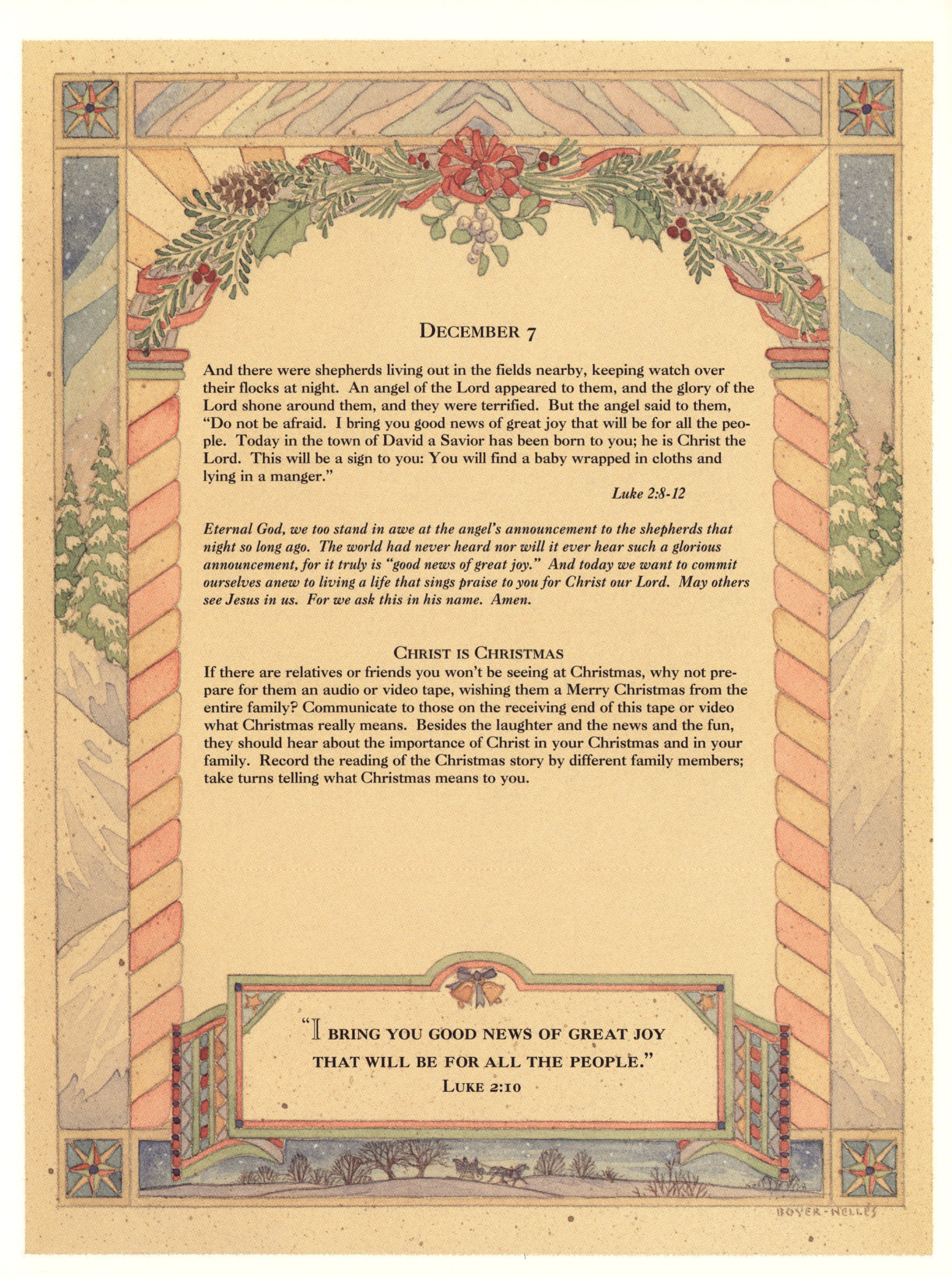

And there were shepherds living out in the fields nearby, keeping watch over their flocks at night. An angel of the Lord appeared to them, and the glory of the Lord shone around them, and they were terrified. But the angel said to them, "Do not be afraid. I bring you good news of great joy that will be for all the people. Today in the town of David a Savior has been born to you; he is Christ the Lord. This will be a sign to you: You will find a baby wrapped in cloths and lying in a manger."

Luke 2:8-12

Eternal God, we too stand in awe at the angel's announcement to the shepherds that night so long ago. The world had never heard nor will it ever hear such a glorious announcement, for it truly is "good news of great joy." And today we want to commit ourselves anew to living a life that sings praise to you for Christ our Lord. May others see Jesus in us. For we ask this in his name. Amen.

Christ is Christmas

If there are relatives or friends you won't be seeing at Christmas, why not prepare for them an audio or video tape, wishing them a Merry Christmas from the entire family? Communicate to those on the receiving end of this tape or video what Christmas really means. Besides the laughter and the news and the fun, they should hear about the importance of Christ in your Christmas and in your family. Record the reading of the Christmas story by different family members; take turns telling what Christmas means to you.

"I BRING YOU GOOD NEWS OF GREAT JOY THAT WILL BE FOR ALL THE PEOPLE."
LUKE 2:10

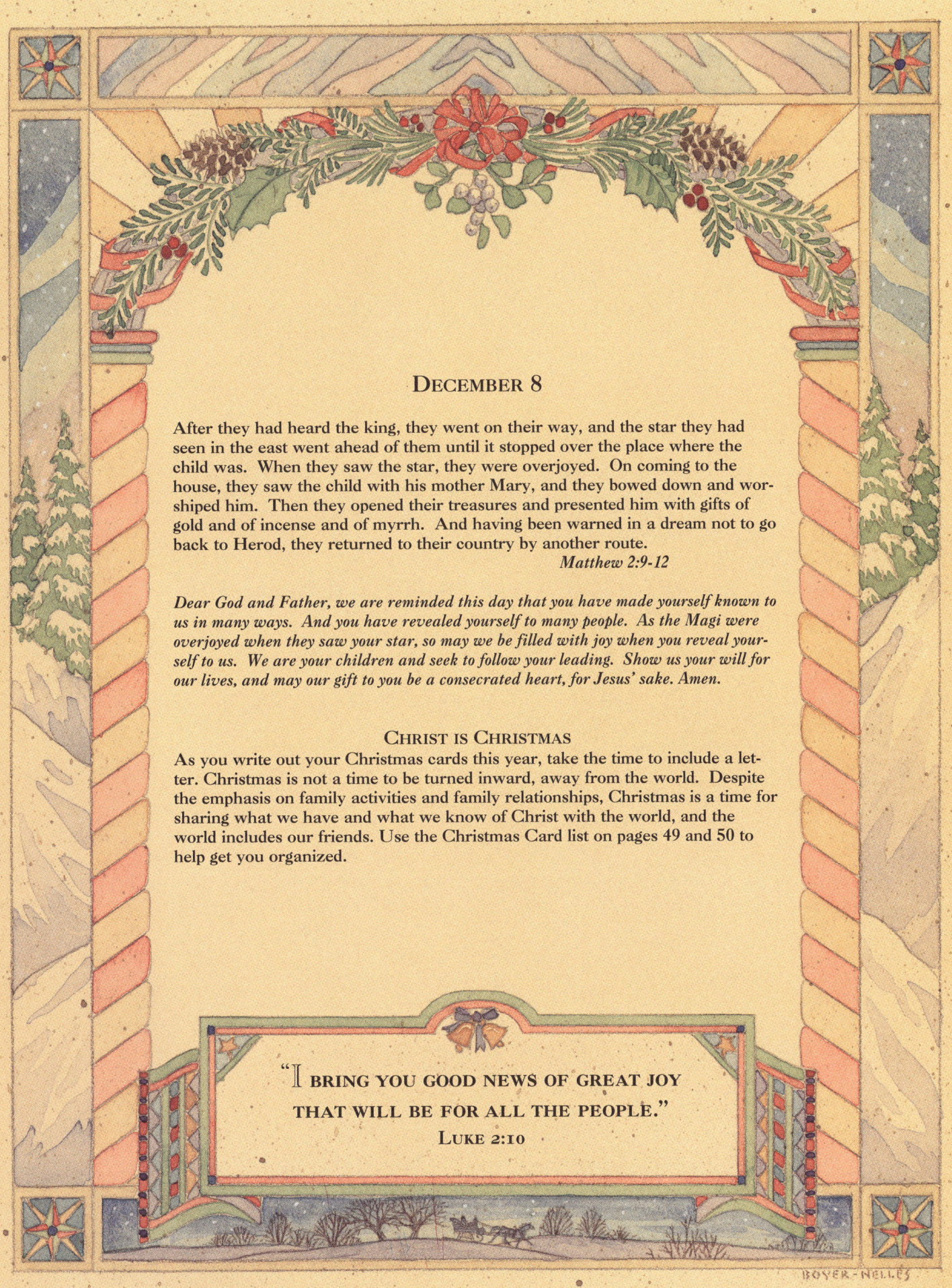

December 8

After they had heard the king, they went on their way, and the star they had seen in the east went ahead of them until it stopped over the place where the child was. When they saw the star, they were overjoyed. On coming to the house, they saw the child with his mother Mary, and they bowed down and worshiped him. Then they opened their treasures and presented him with gifts of gold and of incense and of myrrh. And having been warned in a dream not to go back to Herod, they returned to their country by another route.
Matthew 2:9-12

Dear God and Father, we are reminded this day that you have made yourself known to us in many ways. And you have revealed yourself to many people. As the Magi were overjoyed when they saw your star, so may we be filled with joy when you reveal yourself to us. We are your children and seek to follow your leading. Show us your will for our lives, and may our gift to you be a consecrated heart, for Jesus' sake. Amen.

Christ is Christmas

As you write out your Christmas cards this year, take the time to include a letter. Christmas is not a time to be turned inward, away from the world. Despite the emphasis on family activities and family relationships, Christmas is a time for sharing what we have and what we know of Christ with the world, and the world includes our friends. Use the Christmas Card list on pages 49 and 50 to help get you organized.

> "I bring you good news of great joy that will be for all the people."
> Luke 2:10

December 9

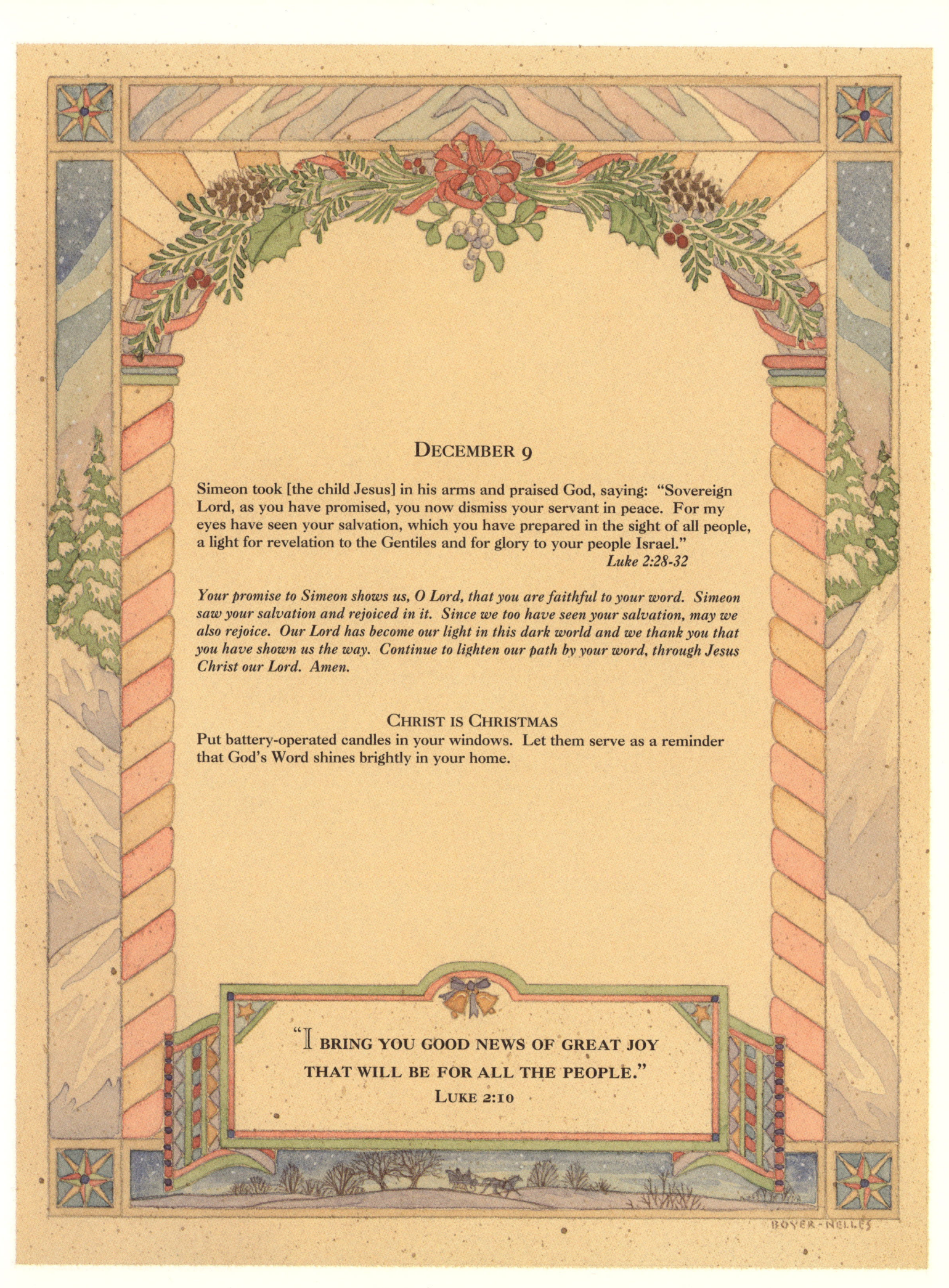

Simeon took [the child Jesus] in his arms and praised God, saying: "Sovereign Lord, as you have promised, you now dismiss your servant in peace. For my eyes have seen your salvation, which you have prepared in the sight of all people, a light for revelation to the Gentiles and for glory to your people Israel."
Luke 2:28-32

Your promise to Simeon shows us, O Lord, that you are faithful to your word. Simeon saw your salvation and rejoiced in it. Since we too have seen your salvation, may we also rejoice. Our Lord has become our light in this dark world and we thank you that you have shown us the way. Continue to lighten our path by your word, through Jesus Christ our Lord. Amen.

Christ is Christmas
Put battery-operated candles in your windows. Let them serve as a reminder that God's Word shines brightly in your home.

"I bring you good news of great joy that will be for all the people."
Luke 2:10

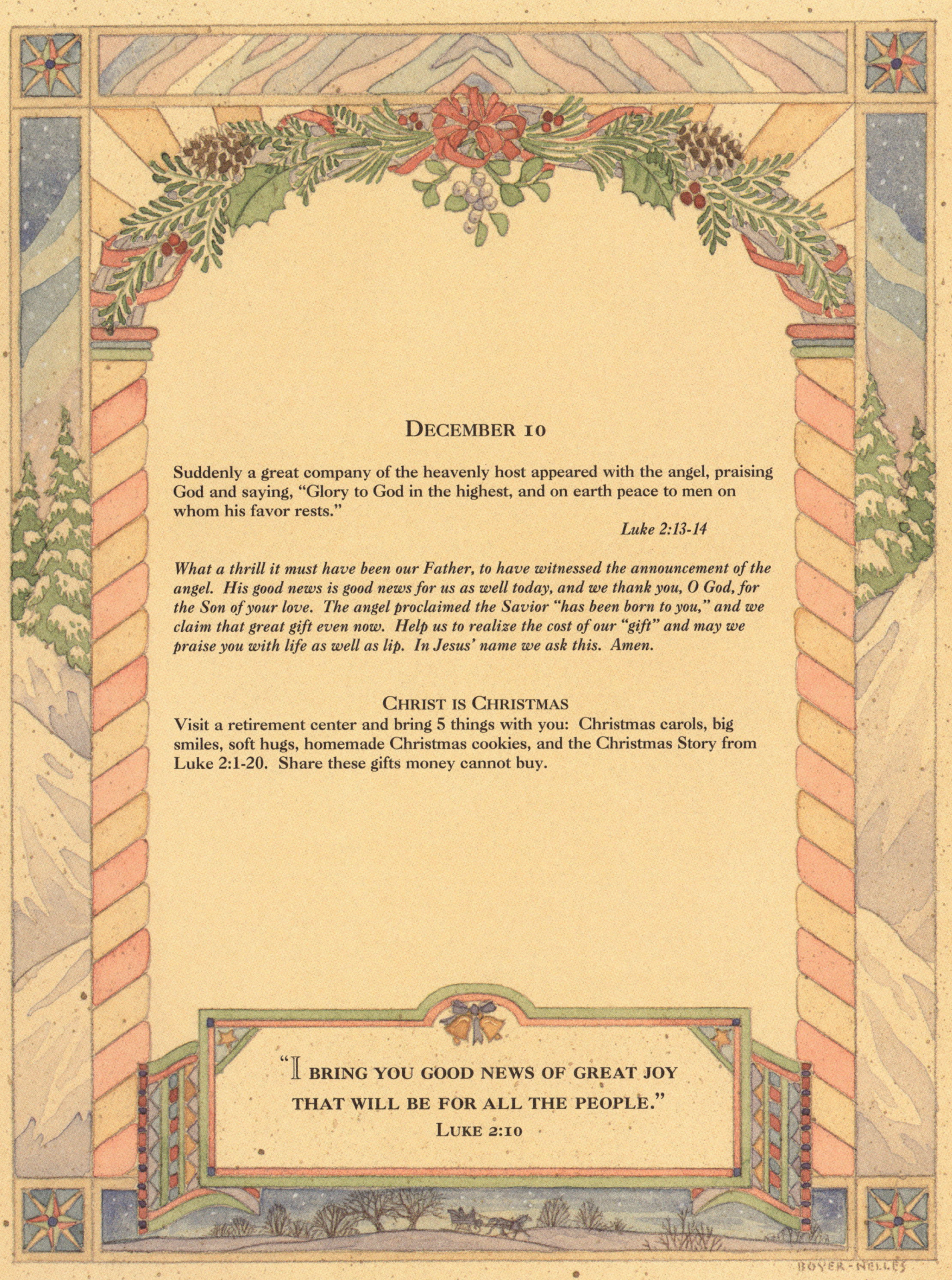

December 10

Suddenly a great company of the heavenly host appeared with the angel, praising God and saying, "Glory to God in the highest, and on earth peace to men on whom his favor rests."

Luke 2:13-14

What a thrill it must have been our Father, to have witnessed the announcement of the angel. His good news is good news for us as well today, and we thank you, O God, for the Son of your love. The angel proclaimed the Savior "has been born to you," and we claim that great gift even now. Help us to realize the cost of our "gift" and may we praise you with life as well as lip. In Jesus' name we ask this. Amen.

Christ is Christmas

Visit a retirement center and bring 5 things with you: Christmas carols, big smiles, soft hugs, homemade Christmas cookies, and the Christmas Story from Luke 2:1-20. Share these gifts money cannot buy.

"I BRING YOU GOOD NEWS OF GREAT JOY THAT WILL BE FOR ALL THE PEOPLE."
LUKE 2:10

December 11

When the angels had left them and gone into heaven, the shepherds said to one another, "Let's go to Bethlehem and see this thing that has happened, which the Lord has told us about."

Luke 2:15

We can understand, O Lord, why the shepherds wanted to go to Bethlehem to see the Savior who had been born. We can only pray today that we may be as eager to understand more about our Savior and his ministry in our lives as the shepherds were to see him. May we cause people to be amazed at what we tell them as to what the Lord means to us. May we impress upon them that what he has done for us he can do for them as well. For Jesus' sake. Amen.

Christ is Christmas

At Christmas, family takes on a wider meaning. Invite anyone you know who won't have a family surrounding them over the holidays. Adopt them as a "relative" and share the message of hope, love and joy. Celebrating the birth of Christ is the perfect introduction to the Gospel.

"I BRING YOU GOOD NEWS OF GREAT JOY THAT WILL BE FOR ALL THE PEOPLE."
LUKE 2:10

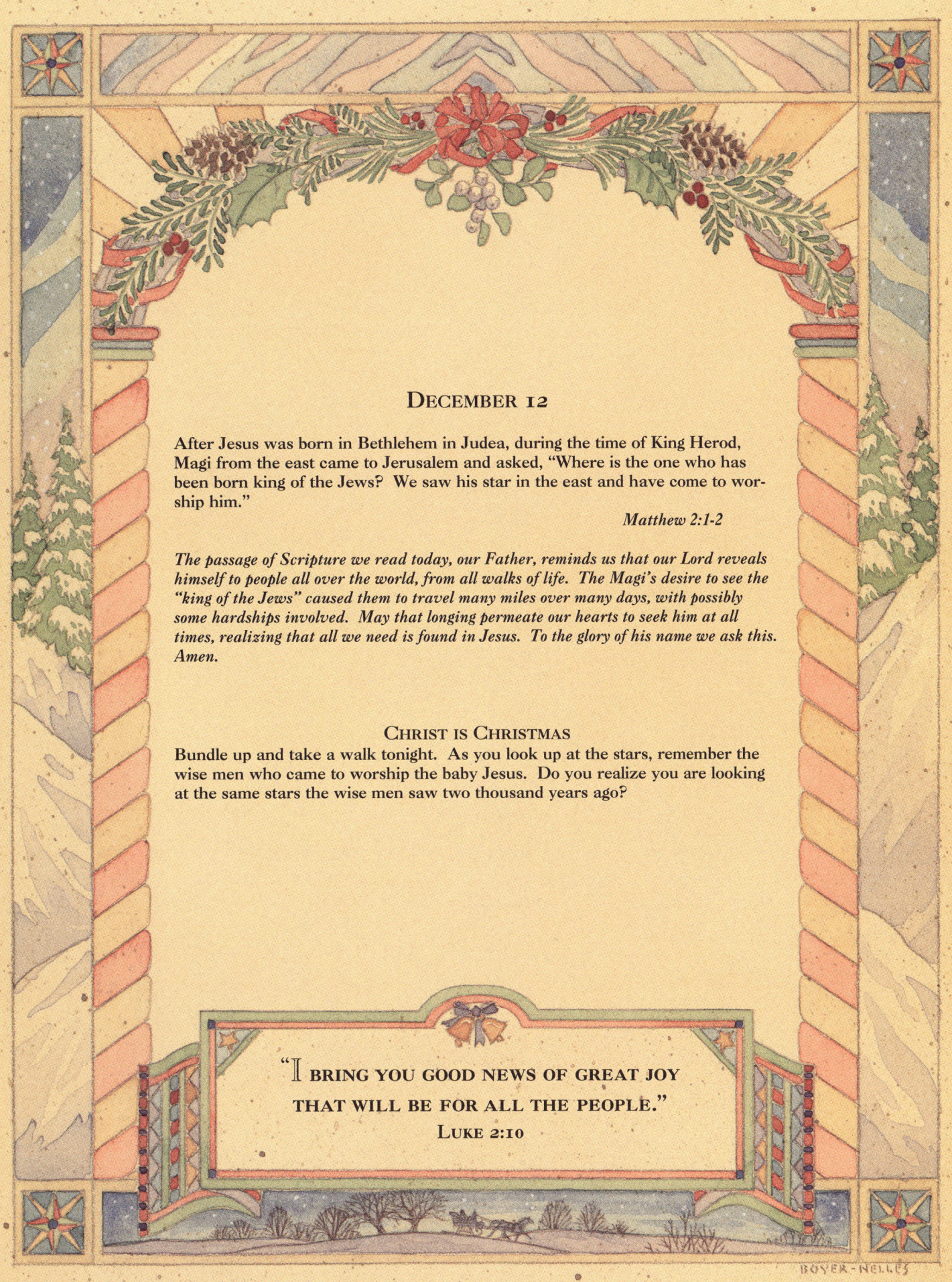

December 12

After Jesus was born in Bethlehem in Judea, during the time of King Herod, Magi from the east came to Jerusalem and asked, "Where is the one who has been born king of the Jews? We saw his star in the east and have come to worship him."

Matthew 2:1-2

The passage of Scripture we read today, our Father, reminds us that our Lord reveals himself to people all over the world, from all walks of life. The Magi's desire to see the "king of the Jews" caused them to travel many miles over many days, with possibly some hardships involved. May that longing permeate our hearts to seek him at all times, realizing that all we need is found in Jesus. To the glory of his name we ask this. Amen.

Christ is Christmas

Bundle up and take a walk tonight. As you look up at the stars, remember the wise men who came to worship the baby Jesus. Do you realize you are looking at the same stars the wise men saw two thousand years ago?

"I BRING YOU GOOD NEWS OF GREAT JOY THAT WILL BE FOR ALL THE PEOPLE."
LUKE 2:10

December 13

So Joseph also went up from the town of Nazareth in Galilee to Judea, to Bethlehem the town of David, because he belonged to the house and line of David. He went there to register with Mary, who was pledged to be married to him and was expecting a child. While they were there, the time came for the baby to be born, and she gave birth to her firstborn, a son. She wrapped him in cloths and placed him in a manger, because there was no room for them in the inn.

Luke 2:4-7

Heavenly Father, we want to remember today two other people who played such an important role in the first Christmas celebration — Mary and Joseph. We know from Scripture that Mary was "highly favored" to become the mother of our Lord, and we are touched by her humility. May that humility be ours when we remember it is by grace we "have been saved—through faith," and it is not from ourselves. We want to thank you again today for your great gift of salvation. In the name of our blessed Lord we pray. Amen.

Christ is Christmas

Build a family tradition around your Christmas manger scene. Begin with figures of Mary, Joseph and Jesus. As a family, construct your own manger, making it traditional in appearance or something unique. Each year, add a figure to the scene. Use the scene to tell the story of Jesus' birth on Christmas Eve.

"I BRING YOU GOOD NEWS OF GREAT JOY THAT WILL BE FOR ALL THE PEOPLE."
LUKE 2:10

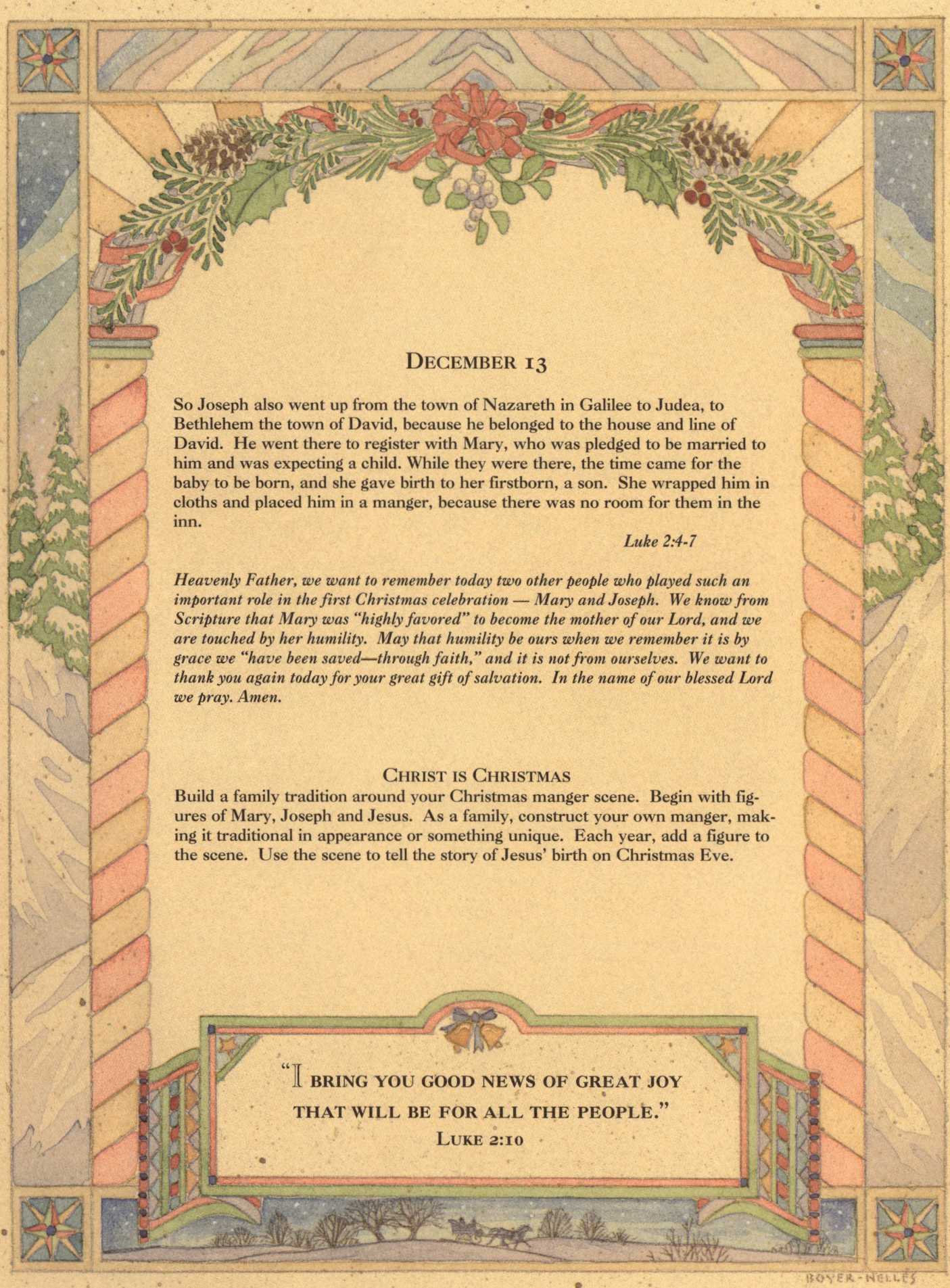

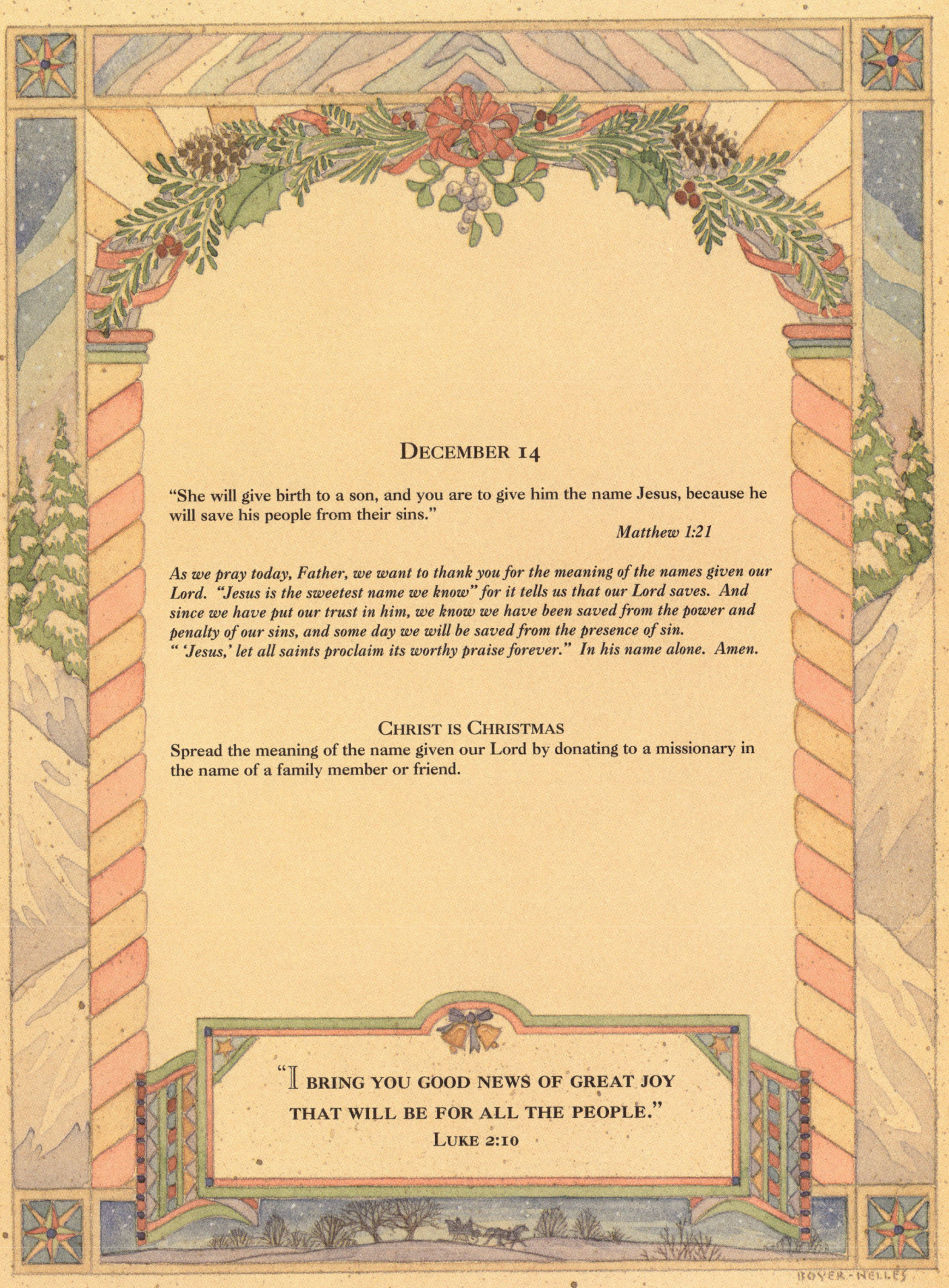

December 14

"She will give birth to a son, and you are to give him the name Jesus, because he will save his people from their sins."

Matthew 1:21

As we pray today, Father, we want to thank you for the meaning of the names given our Lord. "Jesus is the sweetest name we know" for it tells us that our Lord saves. And since we have put our trust in him, we know we have been saved from the power and penalty of our sins, and some day we will be saved from the presence of sin.
" 'Jesus,' let all saints proclaim its worthy praise forever." In his name alone. Amen.

Christ is Christmas

Spread the meaning of the name given our Lord by donating to a missionary in the name of a family member or friend.

"I BRING YOU GOOD NEWS OF GREAT JOY
THAT WILL BE FOR ALL THE PEOPLE."
LUKE 2:10

December 15

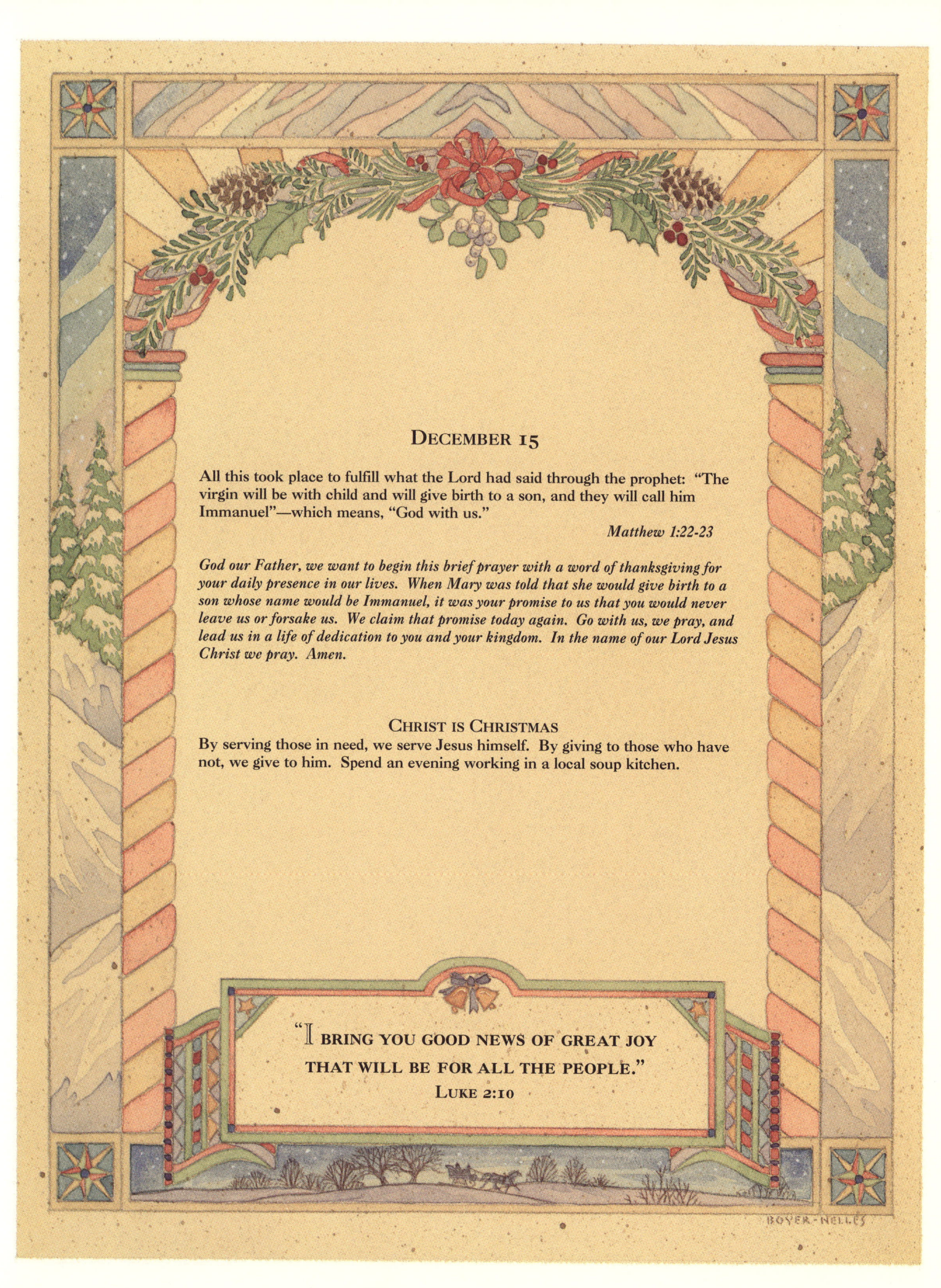

All this took place to fulfill what the Lord had said through the prophet: "The virgin will be with child and will give birth to a son, and they will call him Immanuel"—which means, "God with us."

Matthew 1:22-23

God our Father, we want to begin this brief prayer with a word of thanksgiving for your daily presence in our lives. When Mary was told that she would give birth to a son whose name would be Immanuel, it was your promise to us that you would never leave us or forsake us. We claim that promise today again. Go with us, we pray, and lead us in a life of dedication to you and your kingdom. In the name of our Lord Jesus Christ we pray. Amen.

Christ is Christmas

By serving those in need, we serve Jesus himself. By giving to those who have not, we give to him. Spend an evening working in a local soup kitchen.

"I bring you good news of great joy that will be for all the people."

Luke 2:10

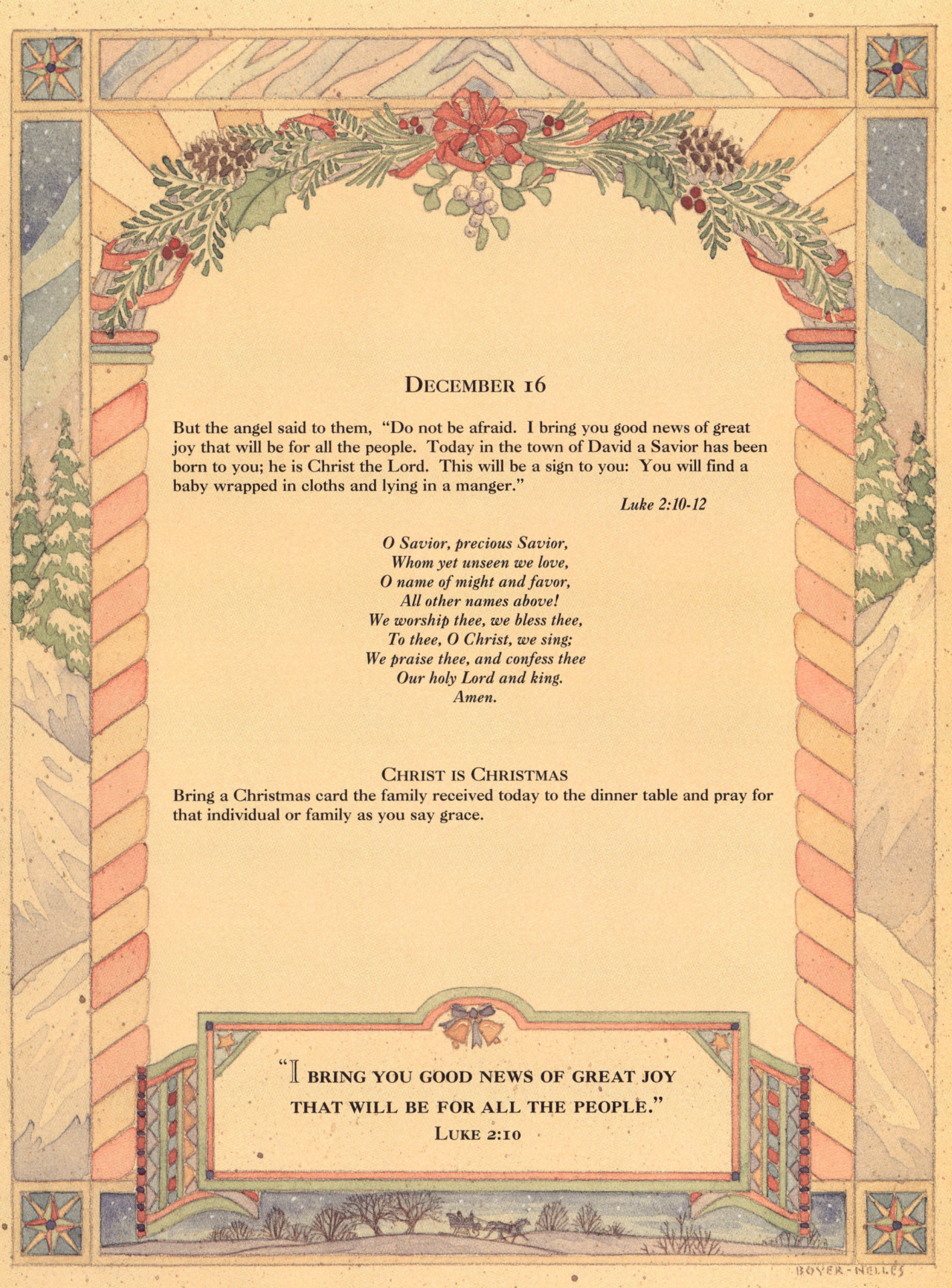

December 16

But the angel said to them, "Do not be afraid. I bring you good news of great joy that will be for all the people. Today in the town of David a Savior has been born to you; he is Christ the Lord. This will be a sign to you: You will find a baby wrapped in cloths and lying in a manger."

Luke 2:10-12

O Savior, precious Savior,
Whom yet unseen we love,
O name of might and favor,
All other names above!
We worship thee, we bless thee,
To thee, O Christ, we sing;
We praise thee, and confess thee
Our holy Lord and king.
Amen.

Christ is Christmas

Bring a Christmas card the family received today to the dinner table and pray for that individual or family as you say grace.

"I bring you good news of great joy that will be for all the people."
Luke 2:10

December 17

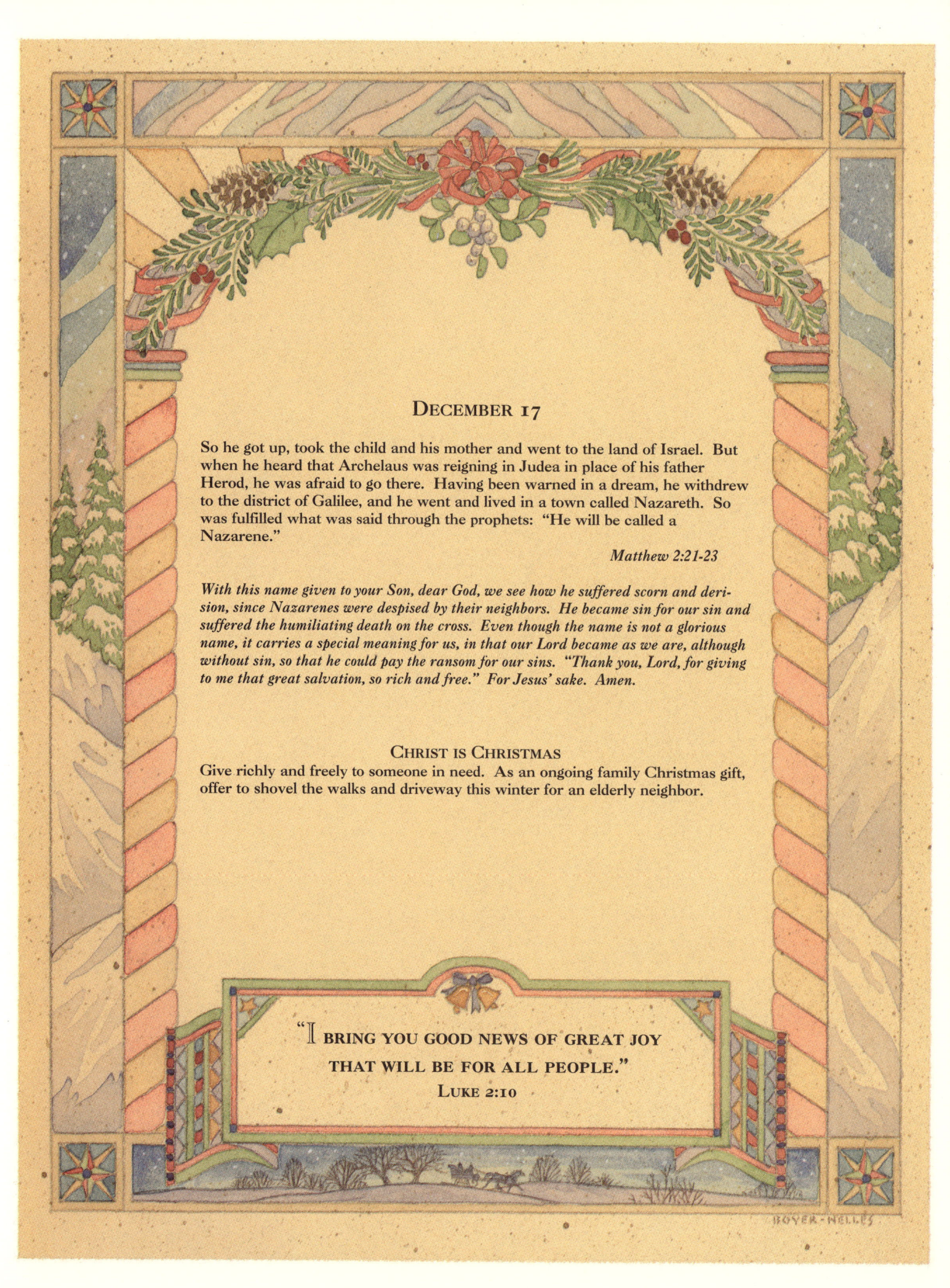

So he got up, took the child and his mother and went to the land of Israel. But when he heard that Archelaus was reigning in Judea in place of his father Herod, he was afraid to go there. Having been warned in a dream, he withdrew to the district of Galilee, and he went and lived in a town called Nazareth. So was fulfilled what was said through the prophets: "He will be called a Nazarene."

Matthew 2:21-23

With this name given to your Son, dear God, we see how he suffered scorn and derision, since Nazarenes were despised by their neighbors. He became sin for our sin and suffered the humiliating death on the cross. Even though the name is not a glorious name, it carries a special meaning for us, in that our Lord became as we are, although without sin, so that he could pay the ransom for our sins. "Thank you, Lord, for giving to me that great salvation, so rich and free." For Jesus' sake. Amen.

Christ is Christmas

Give richly and freely to someone in need. As an ongoing family Christmas gift, offer to shovel the walks and driveway this winter for an elderly neighbor.

"I BRING YOU GOOD NEWS OF GREAT JOY
THAT WILL BE FOR ALL PEOPLE."
LUKE 2:10

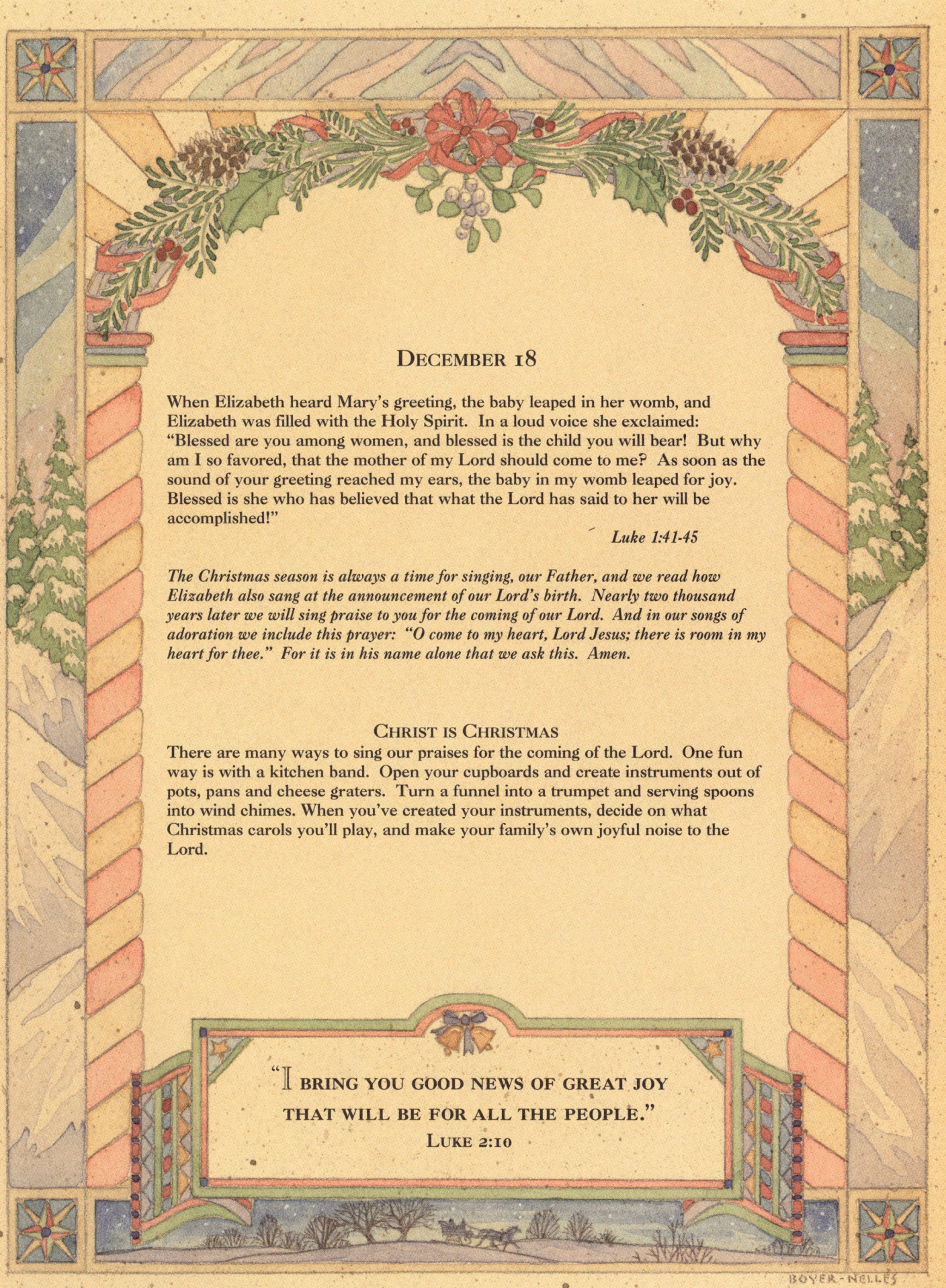

December 18

When Elizabeth heard Mary's greeting, the baby leaped in her womb, and Elizabeth was filled with the Holy Spirit. In a loud voice she exclaimed: "Blessed are you among women, and blessed is the child you will bear! But why am I so favored, that the mother of my Lord should come to me? As soon as the sound of your greeting reached my ears, the baby in my womb leaped for joy. Blessed is she who has believed that what the Lord has said to her will be accomplished!"

Luke 1:41-45

The Christmas season is always a time for singing, our Father, and we read how Elizabeth also sang at the announcement of our Lord's birth. Nearly two thousand years later we will sing praise to you for the coming of our Lord. And in our songs of adoration we include this prayer: "O come to my heart, Lord Jesus; there is room in my heart for thee." For it is in his name alone that we ask this. Amen.

Christ is Christmas

There are many ways to sing our praises for the coming of the Lord. One fun way is with a kitchen band. Open your cupboards and create instruments out of pots, pans and cheese graters. Turn a funnel into a trumpet and serving spoons into wind chimes. When you've created your instruments, decide on what Christmas carols you'll play, and make your family's own joyful noise to the Lord.

"I bring you good news of great joy that will be for all the people."
Luke 2:10

December 19

And Mary said: "My soul glorifies the Lord and my spirit rejoices in God my Savior, for he has been mindful of the humble state of his servant. From now on all generations will call me blessed, for the Mighty One has done great things for me—holy is his name."

Luke 1:46-49

Dear Lord, when Mary in her Song rejoiced that her God was "mindful of the humble state of your servant" we can understand what she meant. She was given a special honor in being chosen the mother of our Lord. We also feel a special honor in being called to salvation and eternal life. You have done great things for us, the greatest being the Christmas gift—the Lord himself. We realize anew today that we were not worthy to the least of your favors, and our spirits rejoice in God our Savior. In his name alone we pray. Amen.

Christ is Christmas

Honor your family's ethnic heritage. Exploring the Christmas traditions of that ethnicity can be great fun, can draw the family closer together, and can also give each of you a greater understanding of Christmas.

"I BRING YOU GOOD NEWS OF GREAT JOY THAT WILL BE FOR ALL THE PEOPLE."
LUKE 2:10

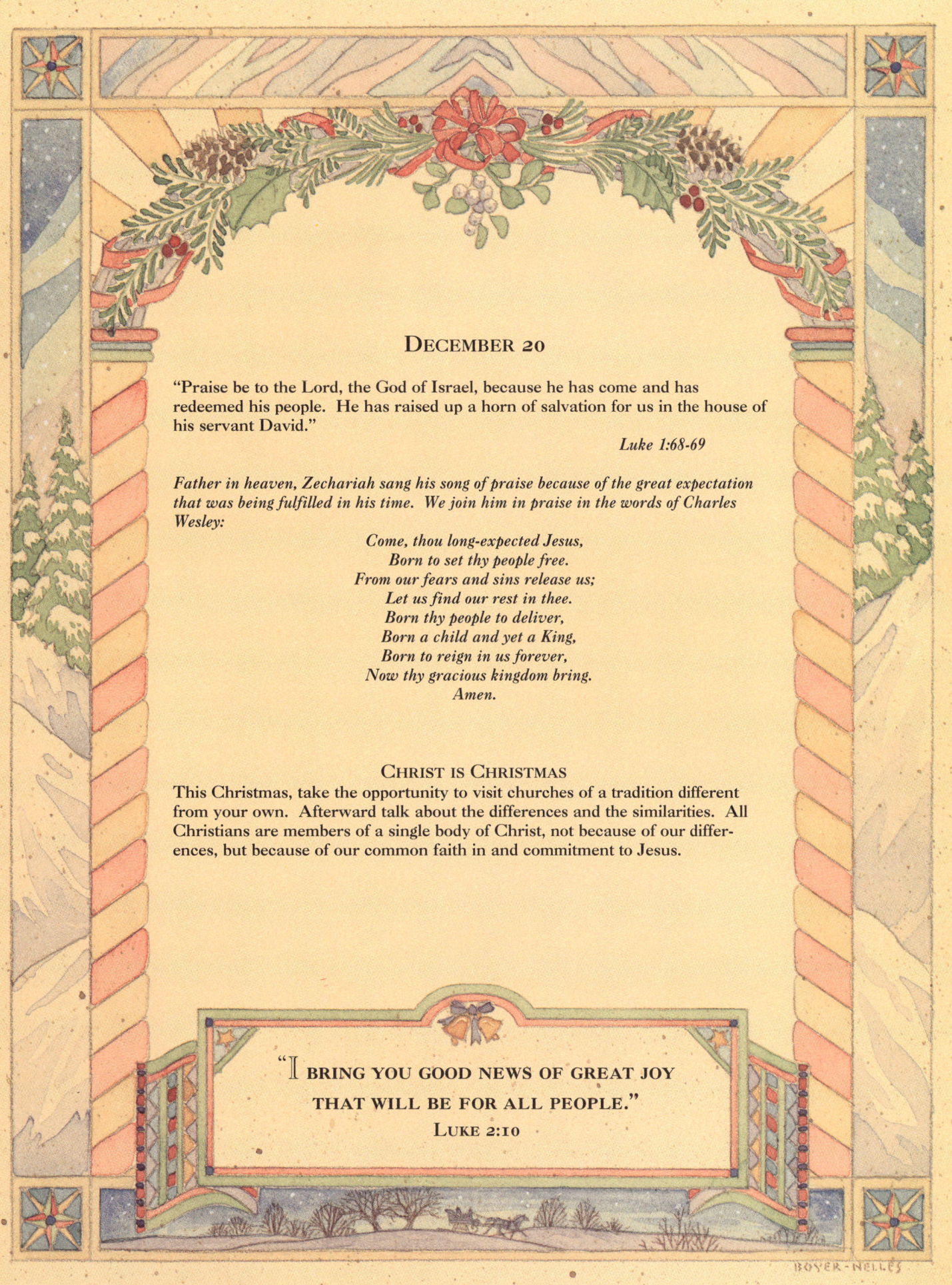

December 20

"Praise be to the Lord, the God of Israel, because he has come and has redeemed his people. He has raised up a horn of salvation for us in the house of his servant David."

Luke 1:68-69

Father in heaven, Zechariah sang his song of praise because of the great expectation that was being fulfilled in his time. We join him in praise in the words of Charles Wesley:

> *Come, thou long-expected Jesus,*
> *Born to set thy people free.*
> *From our fears and sins release us;*
> *Let us find our rest in thee.*
> *Born thy people to deliver,*
> *Born a child and yet a King,*
> *Born to reign in us forever,*
> *Now thy gracious kingdom bring.*
> *Amen.*

Christ is Christmas

This Christmas, take the opportunity to visit churches of a tradition different from your own. Afterward talk about the differences and the similarities. All Christians are members of a single body of Christ, not because of our differences, but because of our common faith in and commitment to Jesus.

"I BRING YOU GOOD NEWS OF GREAT JOY THAT WILL BE FOR ALL PEOPLE."
LUKE 2:10

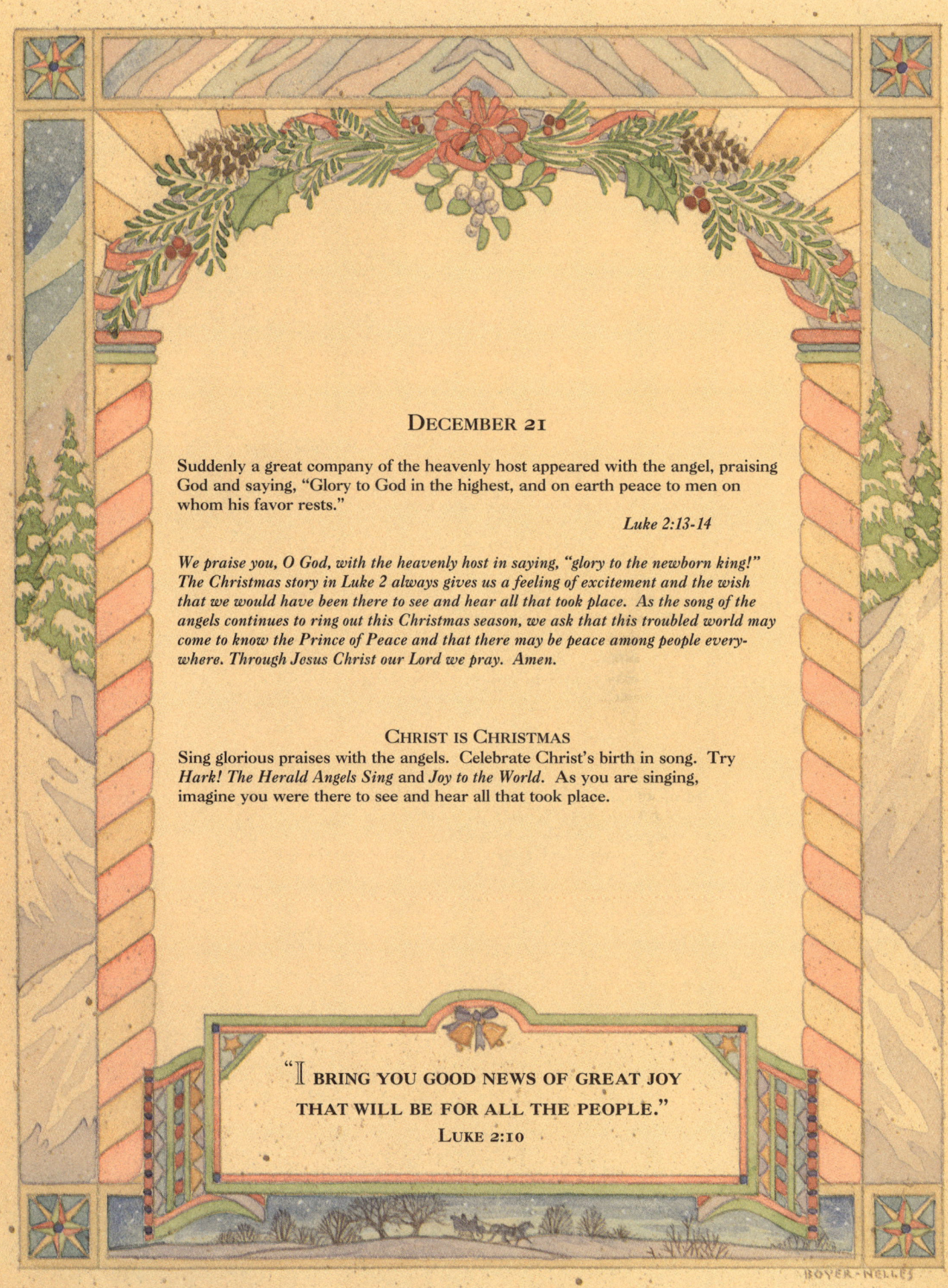

DECEMBER 21

Suddenly a great company of the heavenly host appeared with the angel, praising God and saying, "Glory to God in the highest, and on earth peace to men on whom his favor rests."

Luke 2:13-14

We praise you, O God, with the heavenly host in saying, "glory to the newborn king!" The Christmas story in Luke 2 always gives us a feeling of excitement and the wish that we would have been there to see and hear all that took place. As the song of the angels continues to ring out this Christmas season, we ask that this troubled world may come to know the Prince of Peace and that there may be peace among people everywhere. Through Jesus Christ our Lord we pray. Amen.

CHRIST IS CHRISTMAS

Sing glorious praises with the angels. Celebrate Christ's birth in song. Try *Hark! The Herald Angels Sing* and *Joy to the World*. As you are singing, imagine you were there to see and hear all that took place.

"I BRING YOU GOOD NEWS OF GREAT JOY
THAT WILL BE FOR ALL THE PEOPLE."
LUKE 2:10

December 22

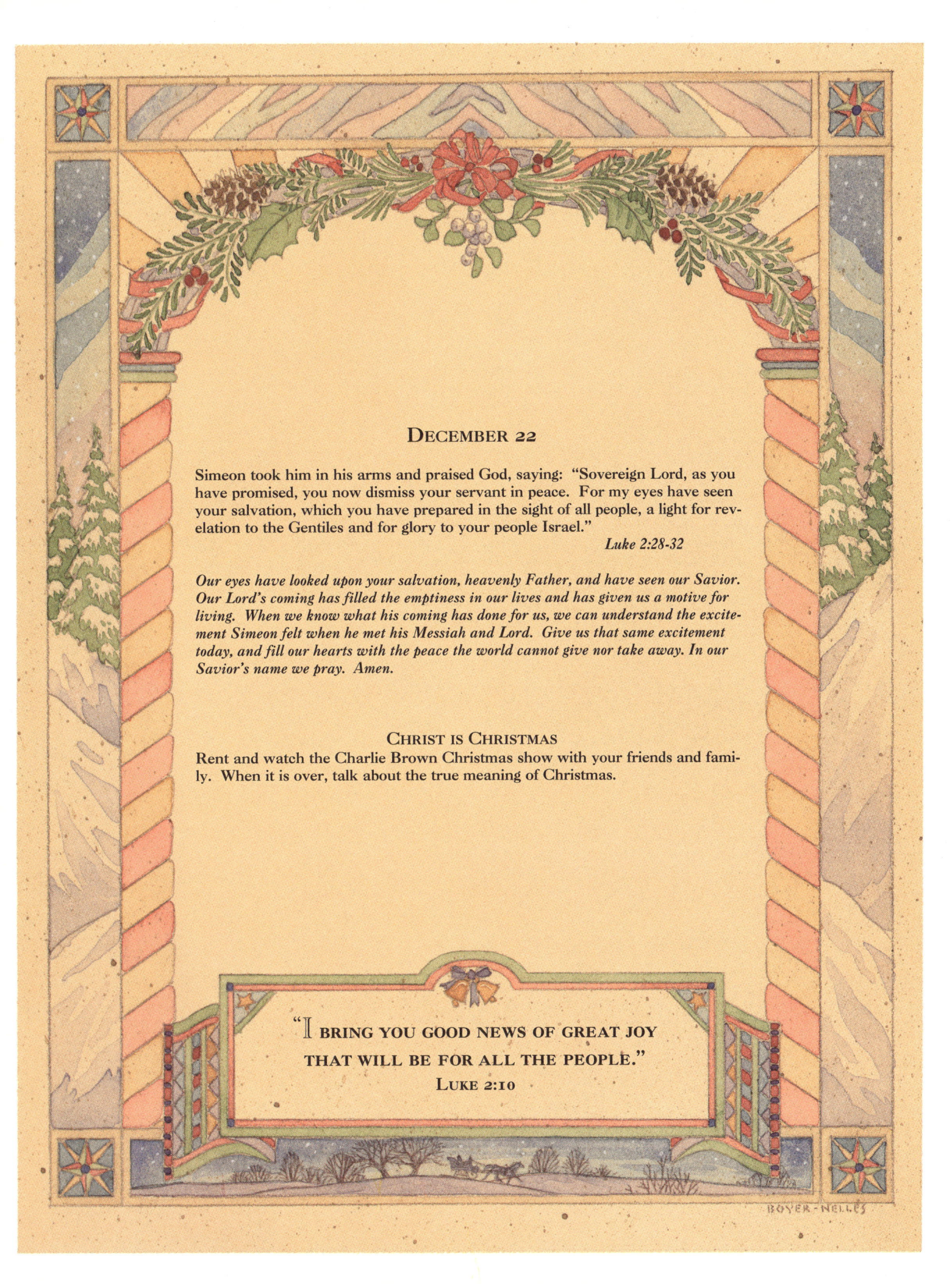

Simeon took him in his arms and praised God, saying: "Sovereign Lord, as you have promised, you now dismiss your servant in peace. For my eyes have seen your salvation, which you have prepared in the sight of all people, a light for revelation to the Gentiles and for glory to your people Israel."
Luke 2:28-32

Our eyes have looked upon your salvation, heavenly Father, and have seen our Savior. Our Lord's coming has filled the emptiness in our lives and has given us a motive for living. When we know what his coming has done for us, we can understand the excitement Simeon felt when he met his Messiah and Lord. Give us that same excitement today, and fill our hearts with the peace the world cannot give nor take away. In our Savior's name we pray. Amen.

Christ is Christmas
Rent and watch the Charlie Brown Christmas show with your friends and family. When it is over, talk about the true meaning of Christmas.

"I BRING YOU GOOD NEWS OF GREAT JOY
THAT WILL BE FOR ALL THE PEOPLE."
LUKE 2:10

December 23

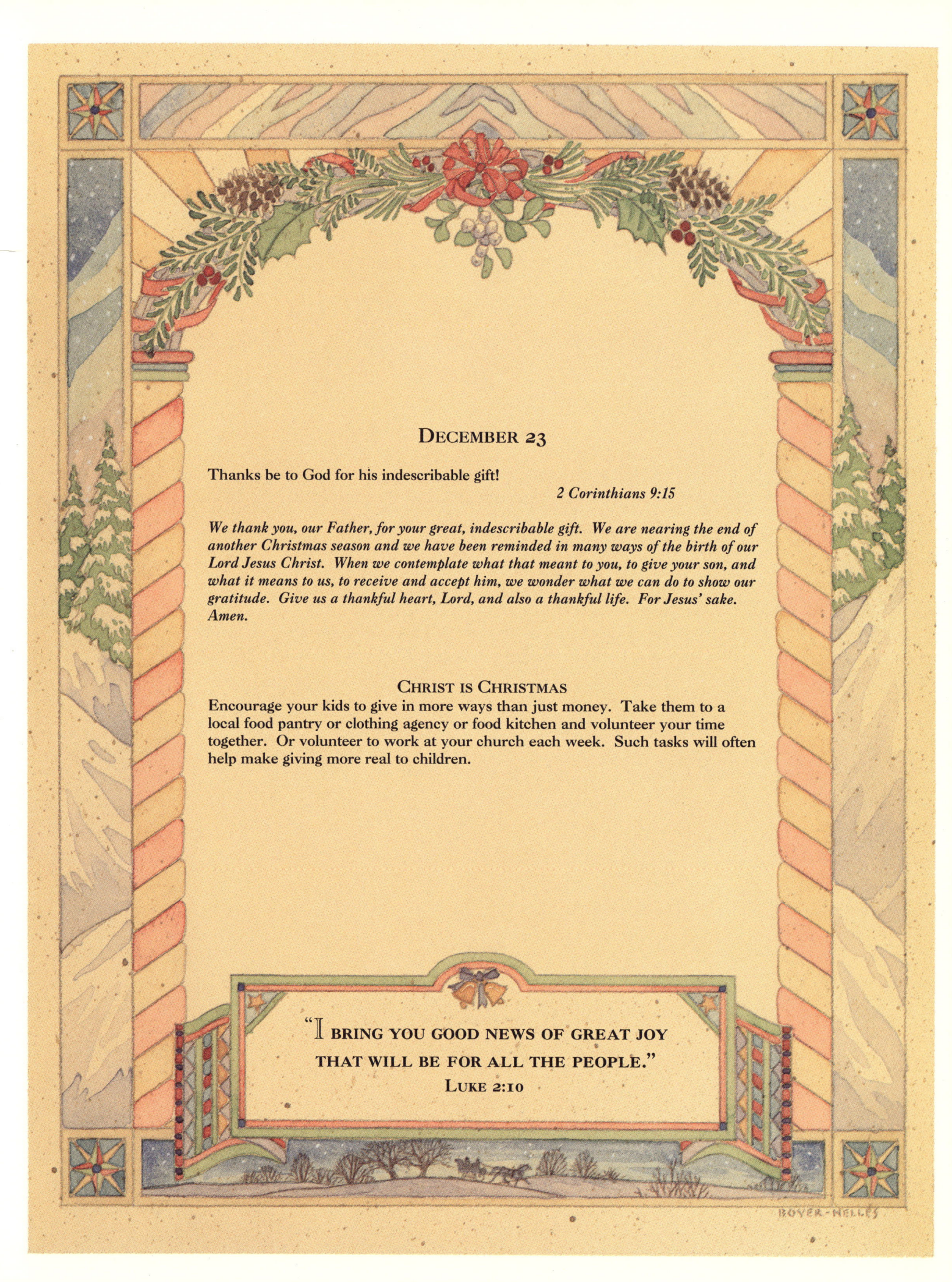

Thanks be to God for his indescribable gift!

2 Corinthians 9:15

We thank you, our Father, for your great, indescribable gift. We are nearing the end of another Christmas season and we have been reminded in many ways of the birth of our Lord Jesus Christ. When we contemplate what that meant to you, to give your son, and what it means to us, to receive and accept him, we wonder what we can do to show our gratitude. Give us a thankful heart, Lord, and also a thankful life. For Jesus' sake. Amen.

Christ is Christmas

Encourage your kids to give in more ways than just money. Take them to a local food pantry or clothing agency or food kitchen and volunteer your time together. Or volunteer to work at your church each week. Such tasks will often help make giving more real to children.

"I BRING YOU GOOD NEWS OF GREAT JOY THAT WILL BE FOR ALL THE PEOPLE."

Luke 2:10

December 24

When they saw the star, they were overjoyed. On coming to the house, they saw the child with his mother Mary, and they bowed down and worshiped him. Then they opened their treasures and presented him with gifts of gold and of incense and of myrrh.

Matthew 2:10-11

Dear Lord, we read in our Scripture lesson that the Magi were overjoyed when they saw the star stop over the place where the Christ child was. And out of joy they worshiped him and presented him with gifts they had brought with them. It was their response that touches our hearts because we too have seen the Lord through the eyes of faith and wish to respond. May the gifts we give the Lord be gifts that come from hearts of love for what we have received through grace, to your honor and glory. Amen.

Christ is Christmas

This Christmas think about the precious gifts given by the wise men—and give Jesus even better ones. Let each member of your family wrap him or herself up as a Christmas present for Jesus. Take pictures of your decorated crew. Talk about what it means to give ourselves to Jesus, to love him and to serve him and others.

"I BRING YOU GOOD NEWS OF GREAT JOY THAT WILL BE FOR ALL THE PEOPLE."
LUKE 2:10

December 25

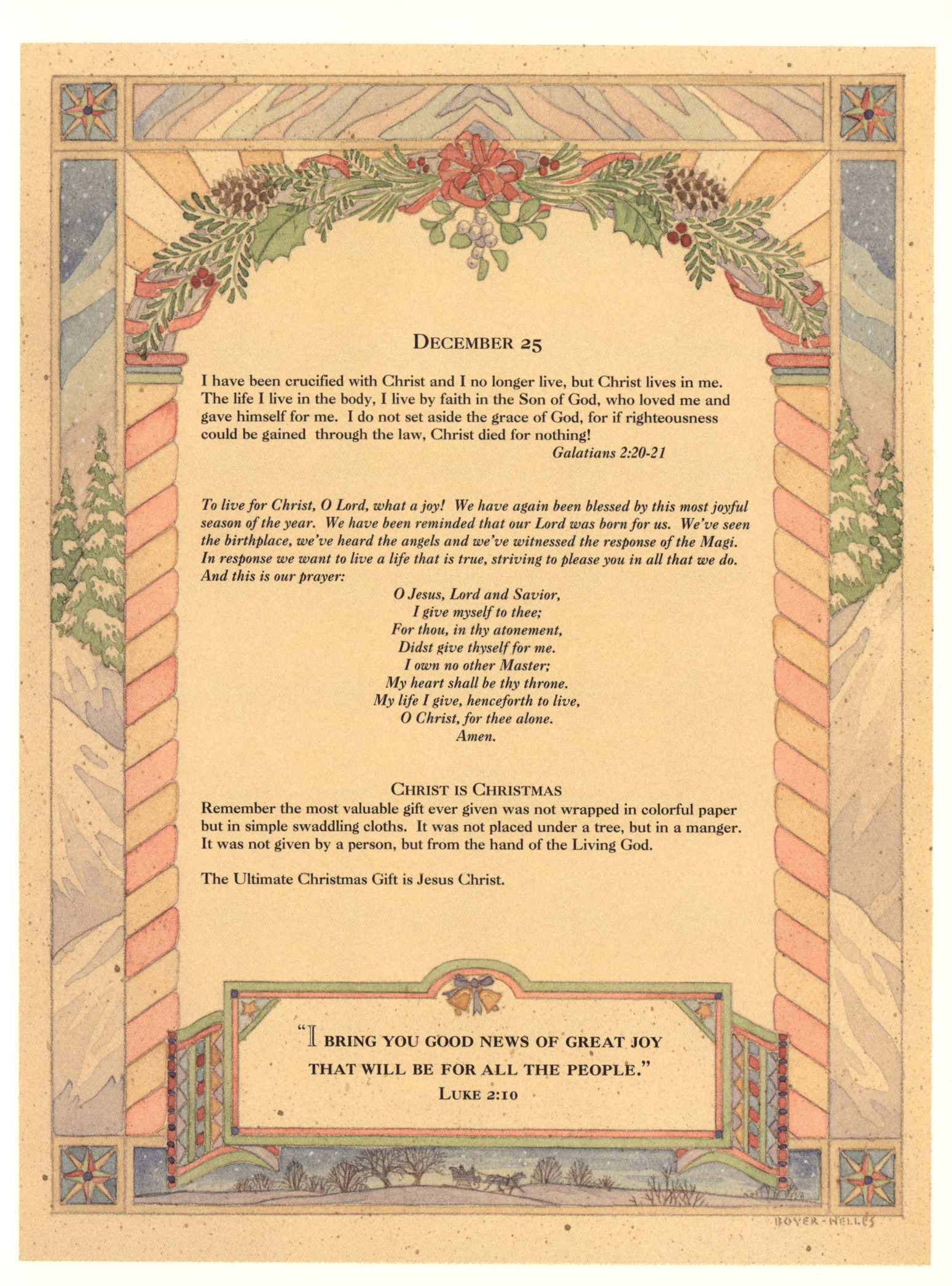

I have been crucified with Christ and I no longer live, but Christ lives in me. The life I live in the body, I live by faith in the Son of God, who loved me and gave himself for me. I do not set aside the grace of God, for if righteousness could be gained through the law, Christ died for nothing!

Galatians 2:20-21

To live for Christ, O Lord, what a joy! We have again been blessed by this most joyful season of the year. We have been reminded that our Lord was born for us. We've seen the birthplace, we've heard the angels and we've witnessed the response of the Magi. In response we want to live a life that is true, striving to please you in all that we do. And this is our prayer:

> O Jesus, Lord and Savior,
> I give myself to thee;
> For thou, in thy atonement,
> Didst give thyself for me.
> I own no other Master;
> My heart shall be thy throne.
> My life I give, henceforth to live,
> O Christ, for thee alone.
> Amen.

Christ is Christmas

Remember the most valuable gift ever given was not wrapped in colorful paper but in simple swaddling cloths. It was not placed under a tree, but in a manger. It was not given by a person, but from the hand of the Living God.

The Ultimate Christmas Gift is Jesus Christ.

"I BRING YOU GOOD NEWS OF GREAT JOY THAT WILL BE FOR ALL THE PEOPLE."

LUKE 2:10

ADVENT REFLECTIONS

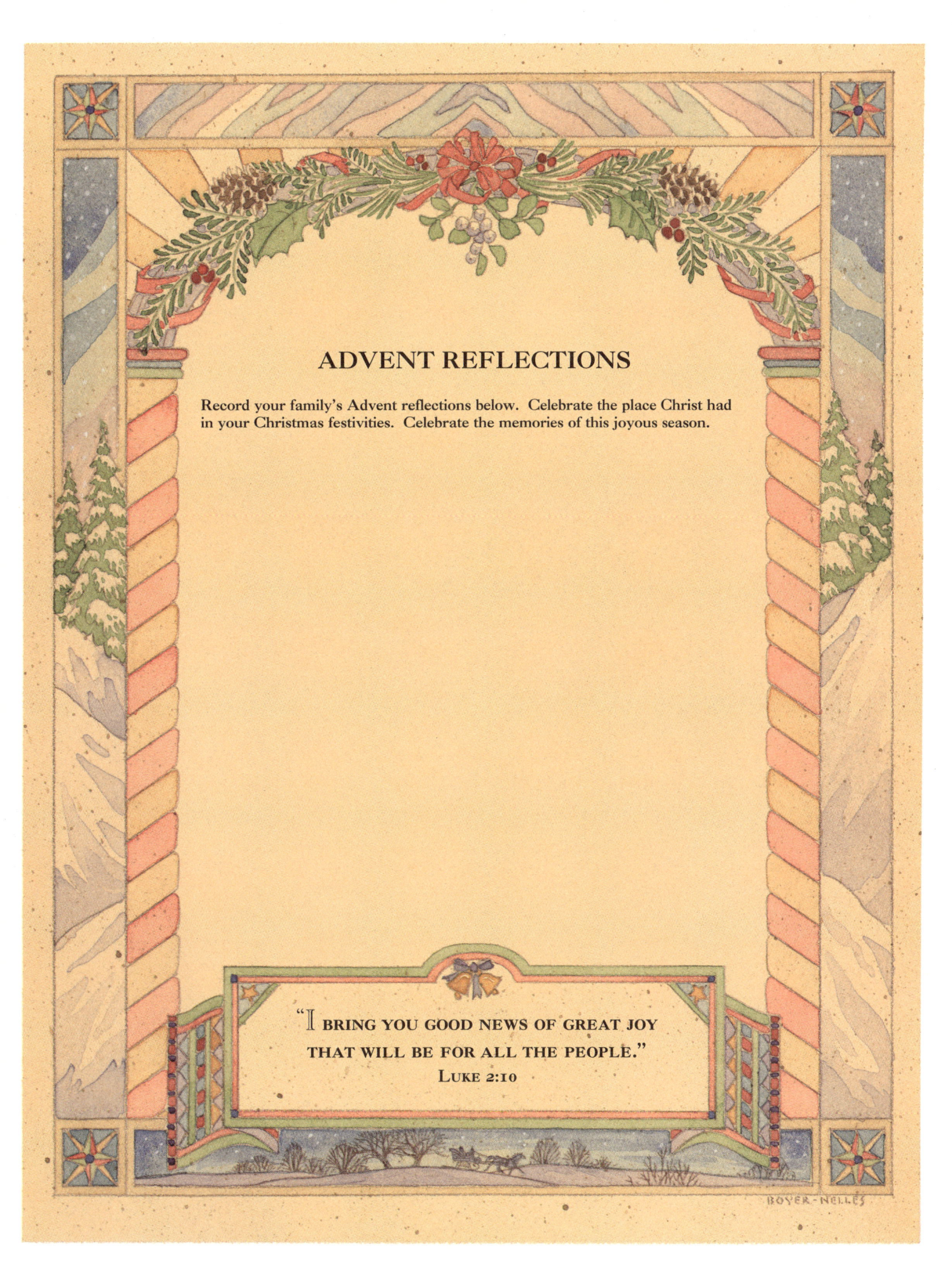

Record your family's Advent reflections below. Celebrate the place Christ had in your Christmas festivities. Celebrate the memories of this joyous season.

"I BRING YOU GOOD NEWS OF GREAT JOY
THAT WILL BE FOR ALL THE PEOPLE."
LUKE 2:10

"For God so loved the world that he gave his one and only Son, that whoever believes in him shall not perish but have eternal life."

John 3:16

The Reason for the Season

"For god so loved the world that he gave his one and only son, that whoever believes in him shall not perish but have eternal life."
John 3:16

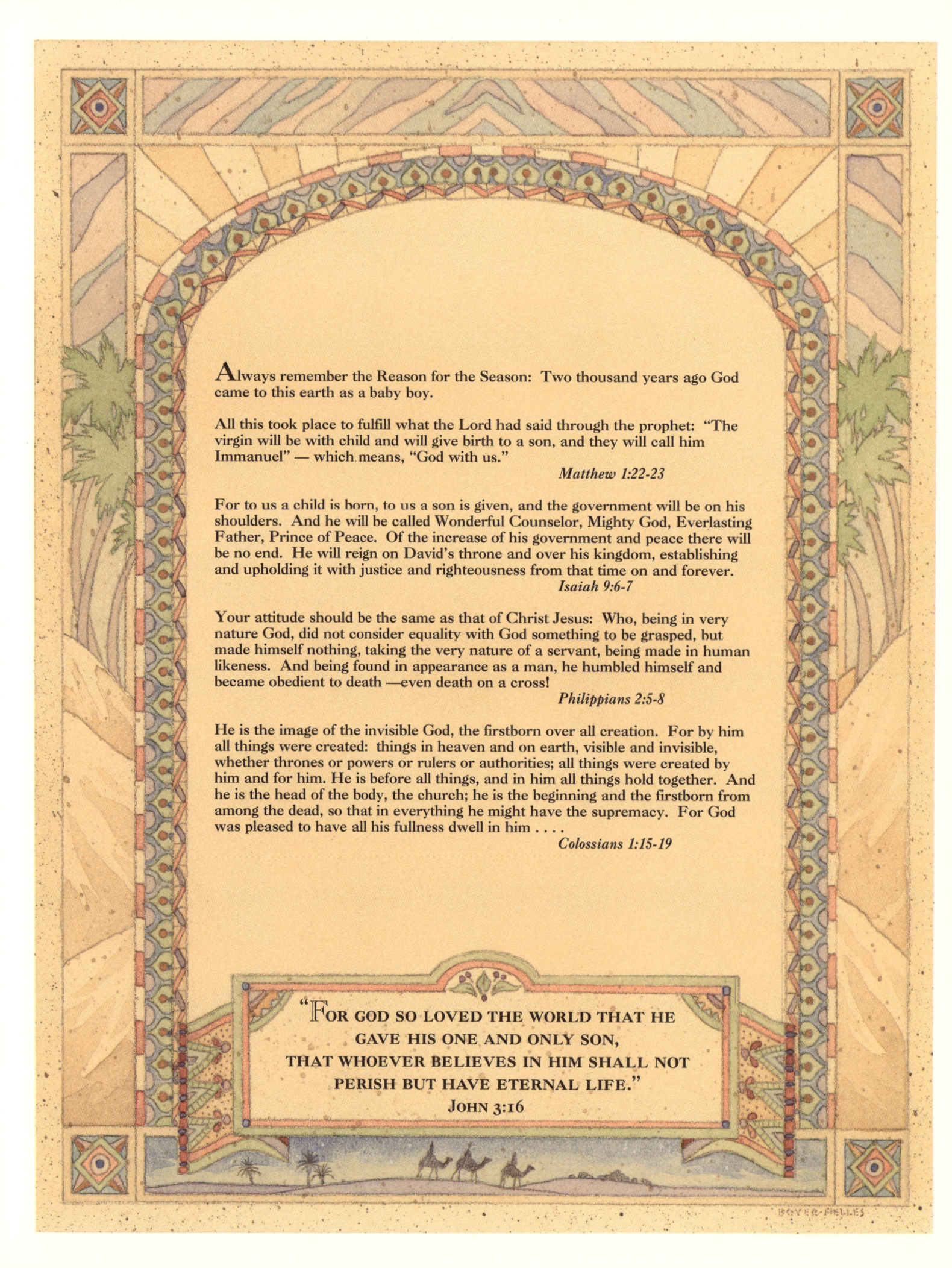

Always remember the Reason for the Season: Two thousand years ago God came to this earth as a baby boy.

All this took place to fulfill what the Lord had said through the prophet: "The virgin will be with child and will give birth to a son, and they will call him Immanuel" — which means, "God with us."

Matthew 1:22-23

For to us a child is born, to us a son is given, and the government will be on his shoulders. And he will be called Wonderful Counselor, Mighty God, Everlasting Father, Prince of Peace. Of the increase of his government and peace there will be no end. He will reign on David's throne and over his kingdom, establishing and upholding it with justice and righteousness from that time on and forever.

Isaiah 9:6-7

Your attitude should be the same as that of Christ Jesus: Who, being in very nature God, did not consider equality with God something to be grasped, but made himself nothing, taking the very nature of a servant, being made in human likeness. And being found in appearance as a man, he humbled himself and became obedient to death —even death on a cross!

Philippians 2:5-8

He is the image of the invisible God, the firstborn over all creation. For by him all things were created: things in heaven and on earth, visible and invisible, whether thrones or powers or rulers or authorities; all things were created by him and for him. He is before all things, and in him all things hold together. And he is the head of the body, the church; he is the beginning and the firstborn from among the dead, so that in everything he might have the supremacy. For God was pleased to have all his fullness dwell in him . . . .

Colossians 1:15-19

"FOR GOD SO LOVED THE WORLD THAT HE
GAVE HIS ONE AND ONLY SON,
THAT WHOEVER BELIEVES IN HIM SHALL NOT
PERISH BUT HAVE ETERNAL LIFE."
JOHN 3:16

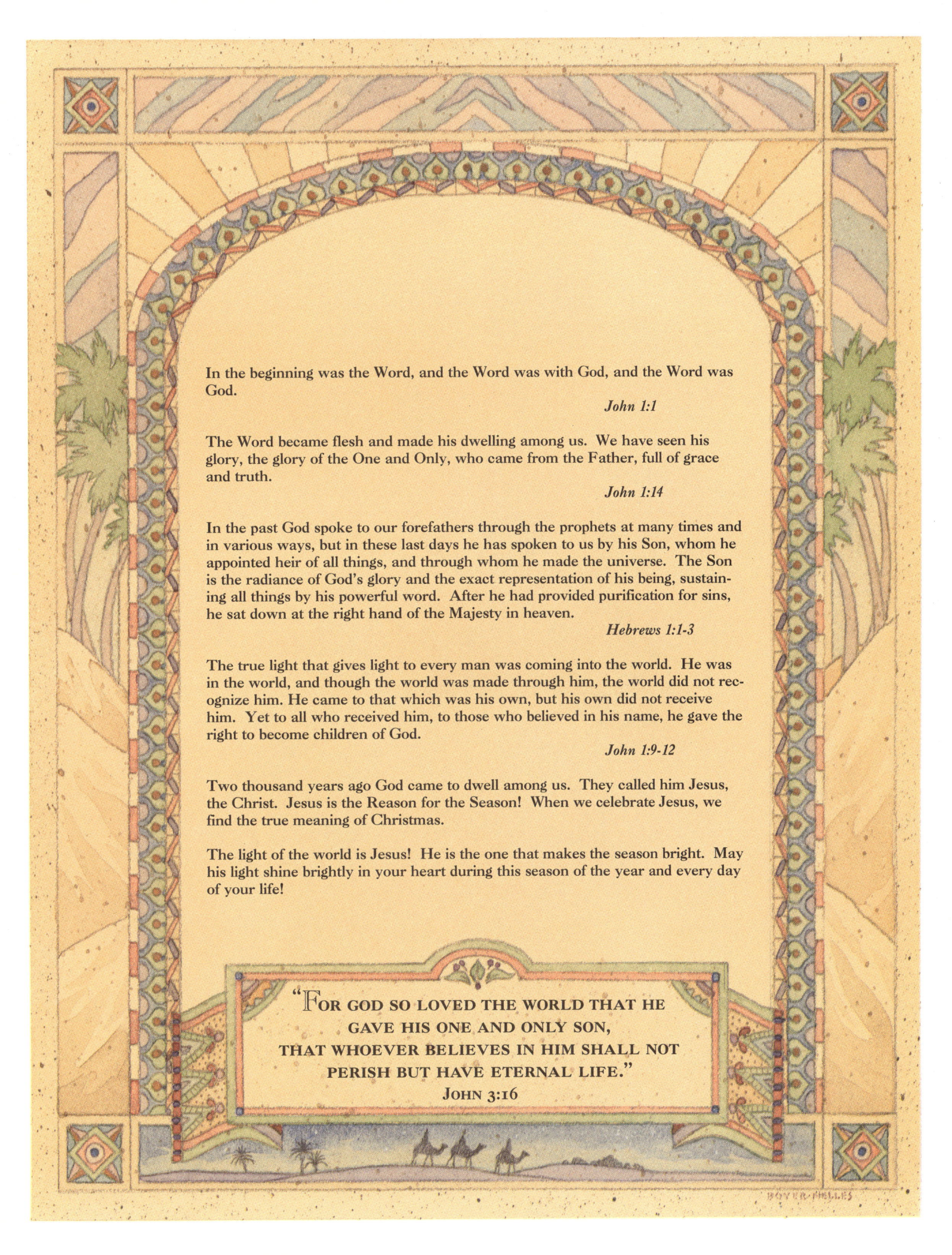

In the beginning was the Word, and the Word was with God, and the Word was God.

John 1:1

The Word became flesh and made his dwelling among us. We have seen his glory, the glory of the One and Only, who came from the Father, full of grace and truth.

John 1:14

In the past God spoke to our forefathers through the prophets at many times and in various ways, but in these last days he has spoken to us by his Son, whom he appointed heir of all things, and through whom he made the universe. The Son is the radiance of God's glory and the exact representation of his being, sustaining all things by his powerful word. After he had provided purification for sins, he sat down at the right hand of the Majesty in heaven.

Hebrews 1:1-3

The true light that gives light to every man was coming into the world. He was in the world, and though the world was made through him, the world did not recognize him. He came to that which was his own, but his own did not receive him. Yet to all who received him, to those who believed in his name, he gave the right to become children of God.

John 1:9-12

Two thousand years ago God came to dwell among us. They called him Jesus, the Christ. Jesus is the Reason for the Season! When we celebrate Jesus, we find the true meaning of Christmas.

The light of the world is Jesus! He is the one that makes the season bright. May his light shine brightly in your heart during this season of the year and every day of your life!

"For god so loved the world that he gave his one and only son, that whoever believes in him shall not perish but have eternal life."

John 3:16

"Thanks be to God for his indescribable gift!"
2 Corinthians 9:15

New Traditions to Begin This Christmas

"Thanks be to God for his indescribable gift!"
2 Corinthians 9:15

- Think of one person who has touched your life in the past year. Sit down and write a letter sharing how their life has blessed yours.

- Buy a basket and some fresh fruit. Arrange your own fruit basket with homemade cards and deliver it to a family in need.

- Attend a Christmas pageant, concert or play in your community or your children's school.

- Plant a small Christmas tree in your yard. Tend this tree each year and when it is big enough, decorate it with lights and share your Christmas cheer with family, friends and neighbors.

- Celebrate Jesus' birthday. Invite family and friends over to the greatest birthday party ever. Serve punch and snacks. Play games. End the evening with a birthday cake and ice cream. Don't forget to sing Happy Birthday to Jesus!

- Hang mistletoe and reinforce your child's sense of belonging with plenty of sloppy kisses.

- Bake homemade cookies with your family or a group of friends and bring them as gifts to elderly people in your church or neighborhood.

- Conduct a gift-giving ceremony for the one whose birthday it is. Each family member writes on a piece of paper what he or she will give to Christ this year. Then fold the papers and place, one at a time, at the feet of Christ beside the manger. The gifts should represent effort or value on our part and be something we feel would please Christ.

- Let music become the background for all of your Christmas activities. And not just the recorded versions, either. Sing! And if you can't sing, whistle!

"THANKS BE TO GOD FOR HIS INDESCRIBABLE GIFT!"
2 CORINTHIANS 9:15

Other new traditions we started this year:

Record other new traditions your family started this year. Capture the memories, the responses and feelings evoked from participating in these meaningful, Christ-filled activities.

"THANKS BE TO GOD FOR HIS
INDESCRIBABLE GIFT!"
2 CORINTHIANS 9:15

"It is more blessed to give than to receive."
Acts 20:35

Old Traditions Enjoyed Anew!

"It is more blessed to give than to receive."
Acts 20:35

CHRISTMAS CARDS

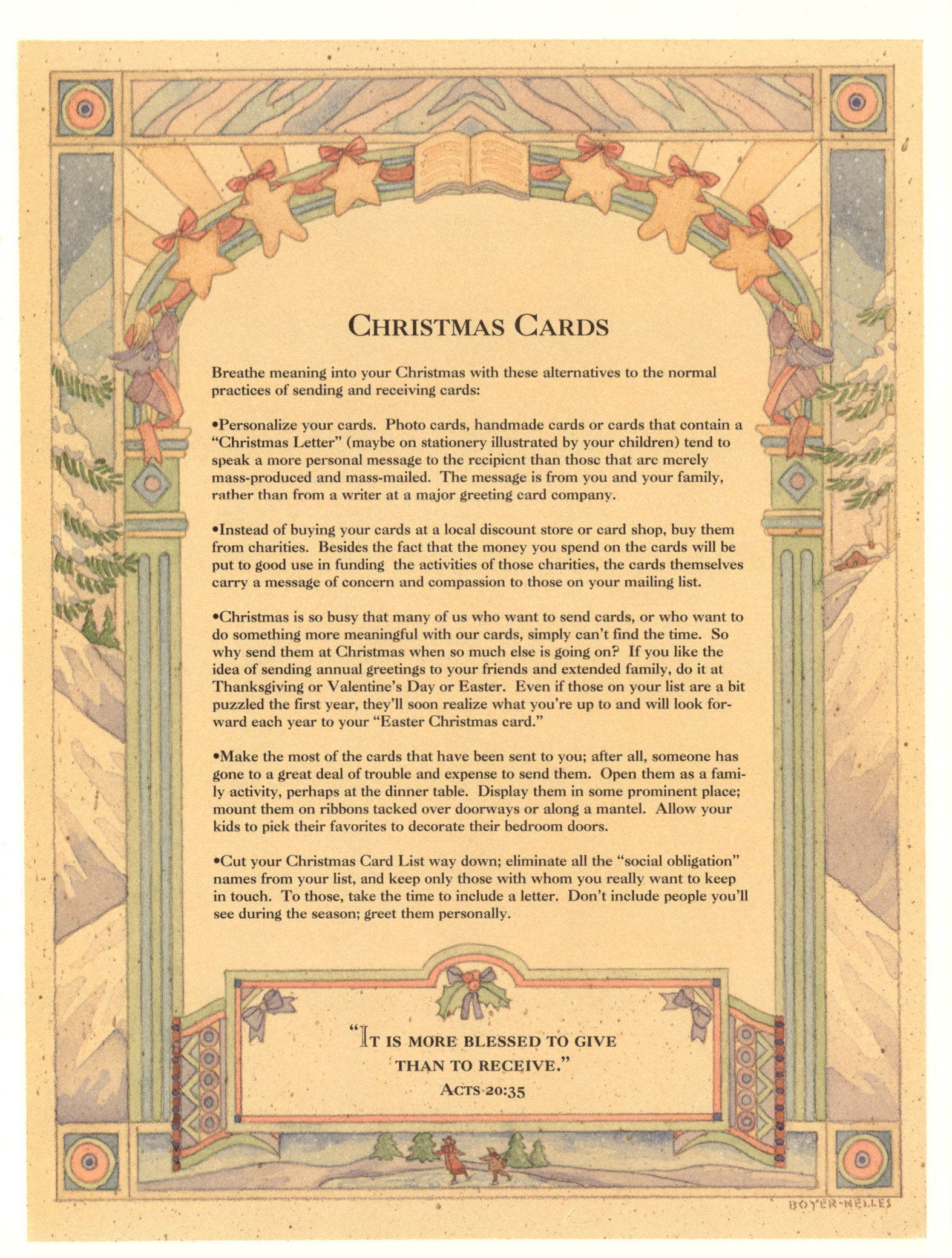

Breathe meaning into your Christmas with these alternatives to the normal practices of sending and receiving cards:

•Personalize your cards. Photo cards, handmade cards or cards that contain a "Christmas Letter" (maybe on stationery illustrated by your children) tend to speak a more personal message to the recipient than those that are merely mass-produced and mass-mailed. The message is from you and your family, rather than from a writer at a major greeting card company.

•Instead of buying your cards at a local discount store or card shop, buy them from charities. Besides the fact that the money you spend on the cards will be put to good use in funding the activities of those charities, the cards themselves carry a message of concern and compassion to those on your mailing list.

•Christmas is so busy that many of us who want to send cards, or who want to do something more meaningful with our cards, simply can't find the time. So why send them at Christmas when so much else is going on? If you like the idea of sending annual greetings to your friends and extended family, do it at Thanksgiving or Valentine's Day or Easter. Even if those on your list are a bit puzzled the first year, they'll soon realize what you're up to and will look forward each year to your "Easter Christmas card."

•Make the most of the cards that have been sent to you; after all, someone has gone to a great deal of trouble and expense to send them. Open them as a family activity, perhaps at the dinner table. Display them in some prominent place; mount them on ribbons tacked over doorways or along a mantel. Allow your kids to pick their favorites to decorate their bedroom doors.

•Cut your Christmas Card List way down; eliminate all the "social obligation" names from your list, and keep only those with whom you really want to keep in touch. To those, take the time to include a letter. Don't include people you'll see during the season; greet them personally.

"IT IS MORE BLESSED TO GIVE
THAN TO RECEIVE."
ACTS 20:35

Christmas Card List

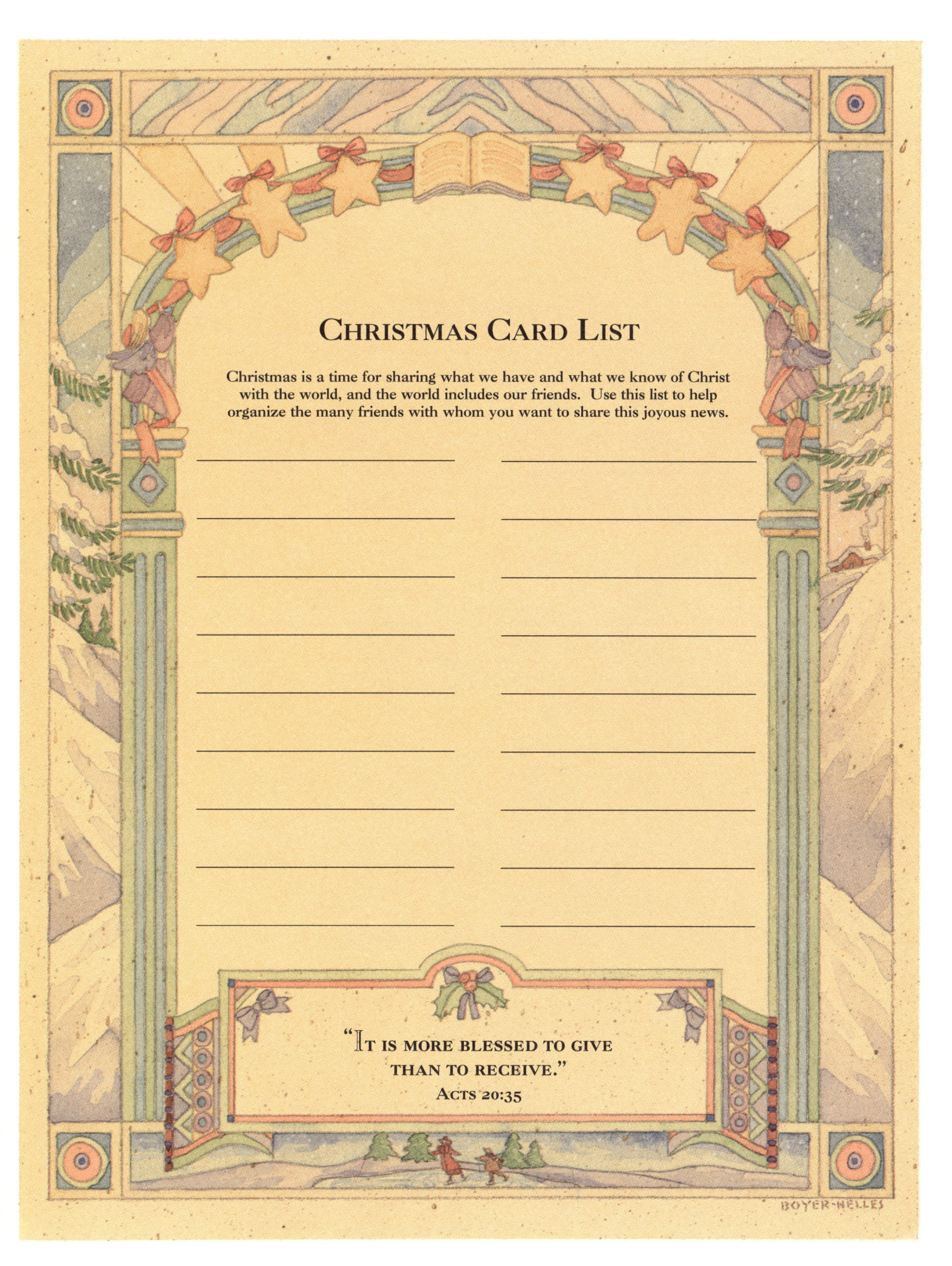

Christmas is a time for sharing what we have and what we know of Christ with the world, and the world includes our friends. Use this list to help organize the many friends with whom you want to share this joyous news.

_____   _____

_____   _____

_____   _____

_____   _____

_____   _____

_____   _____

_____   _____

_____   _____

"It is more blessed to give than to receive."
Acts 20:35

Christmas Card List

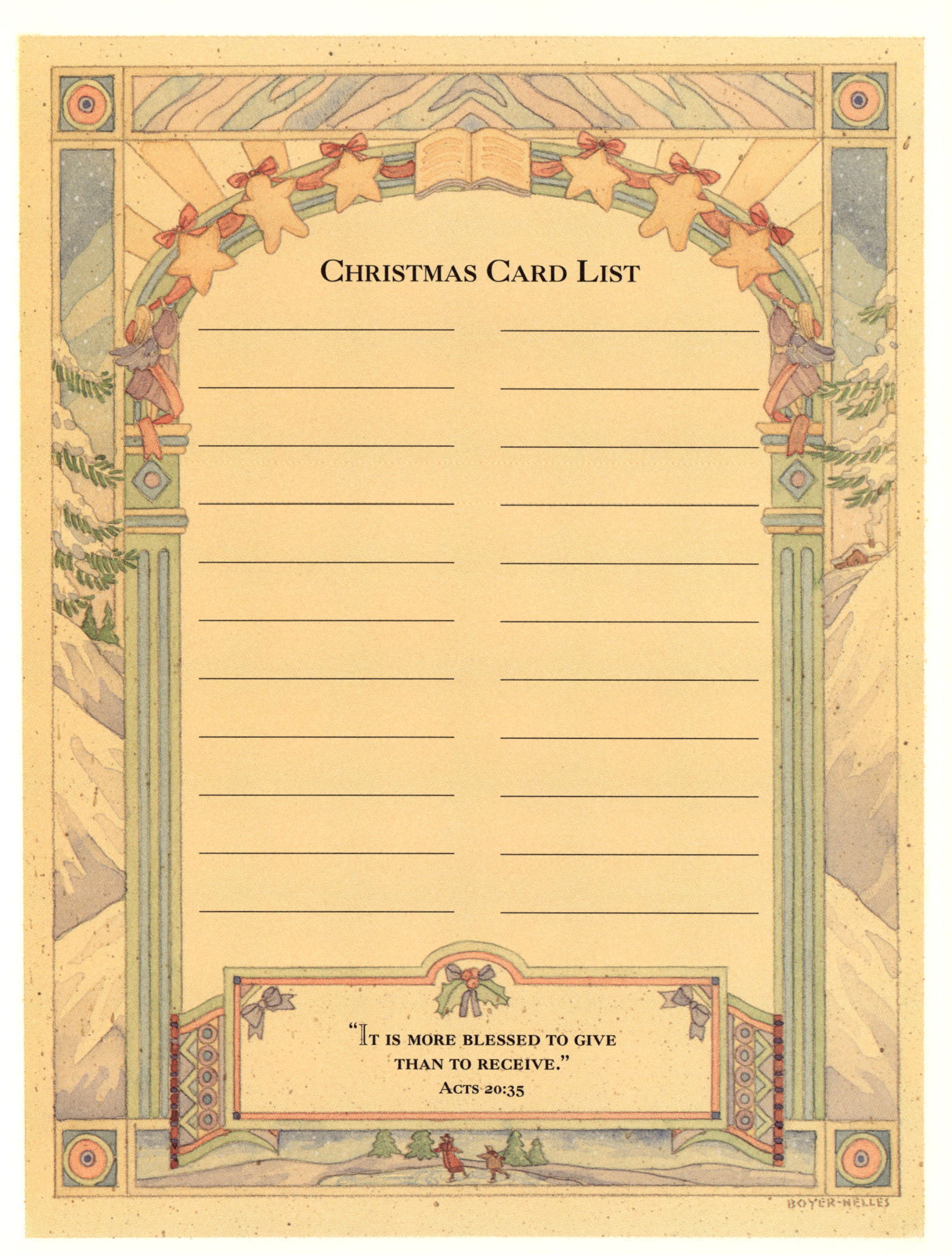

_____   _____
_____   _____
_____   _____
_____   _____
_____   _____
_____   _____
_____   _____
_____   _____
_____   _____
_____   _____

"It is more blessed to give
than to receive."
Acts 20:35

CHRISTMAS GIFTS

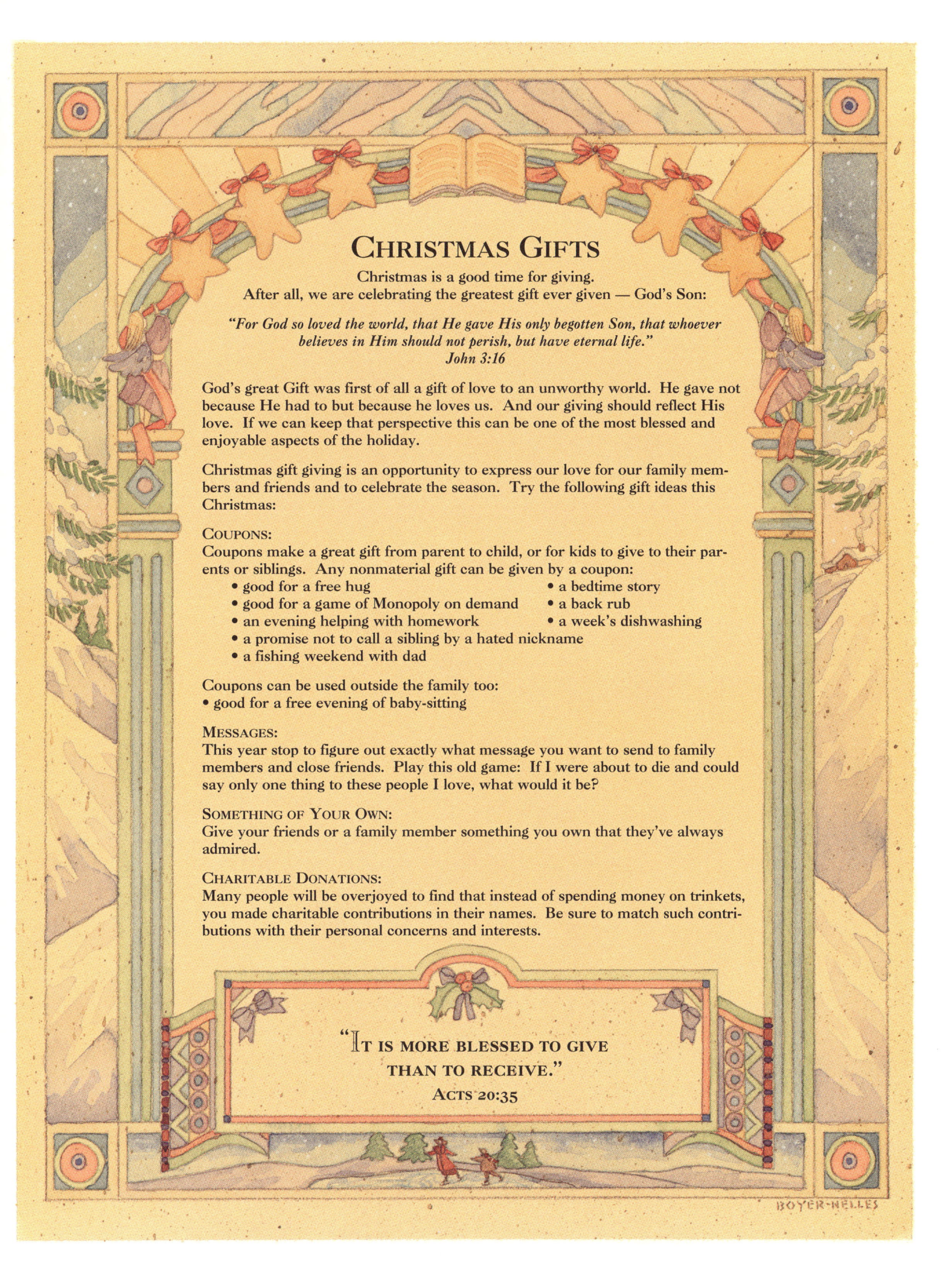

Christmas is a good time for giving.
After all, we are celebrating the greatest gift ever given — God's Son:

"For God so loved the world, that He gave His only begotten Son, that whoever believes in Him should not perish, but have eternal life."
John 3:16

God's great Gift was first of all a gift of love to an unworthy world. He gave not because He had to but because he loves us. And our giving should reflect His love. If we can keep that perspective this can be one of the most blessed and enjoyable aspects of the holiday.

Christmas gift giving is an opportunity to express our love for our family members and friends and to celebrate the season. Try the following gift ideas this Christmas:

COUPONS:
Coupons make a great gift from parent to child, or for kids to give to their parents or siblings. Any nonmaterial gift can be given by a coupon:
- good for a free hug
- good for a game of Monopoly on demand
- an evening helping with homework
- a promise not to call a sibling by a hated nickname
- a fishing weekend with dad
- a bedtime story
- a back rub
- a week's dishwashing

Coupons can be used outside the family too:
- good for a free evening of baby-sitting

MESSAGES:
This year stop to figure out exactly what message you want to send to family members and close friends. Play this old game: If I were about to die and could say only one thing to these people I love, what would it be?

SOMETHING OF YOUR OWN:
Give your friends or a family member something you own that they've always admired.

CHARITABLE DONATIONS:
Many people will be overjoyed to find that instead of spending money on trinkets, you made charitable contributions in their names. Be sure to match such contributions with their personal concerns and interests.

"It is more blessed to give than to receive."
Acts 20:35

Christmas Gift

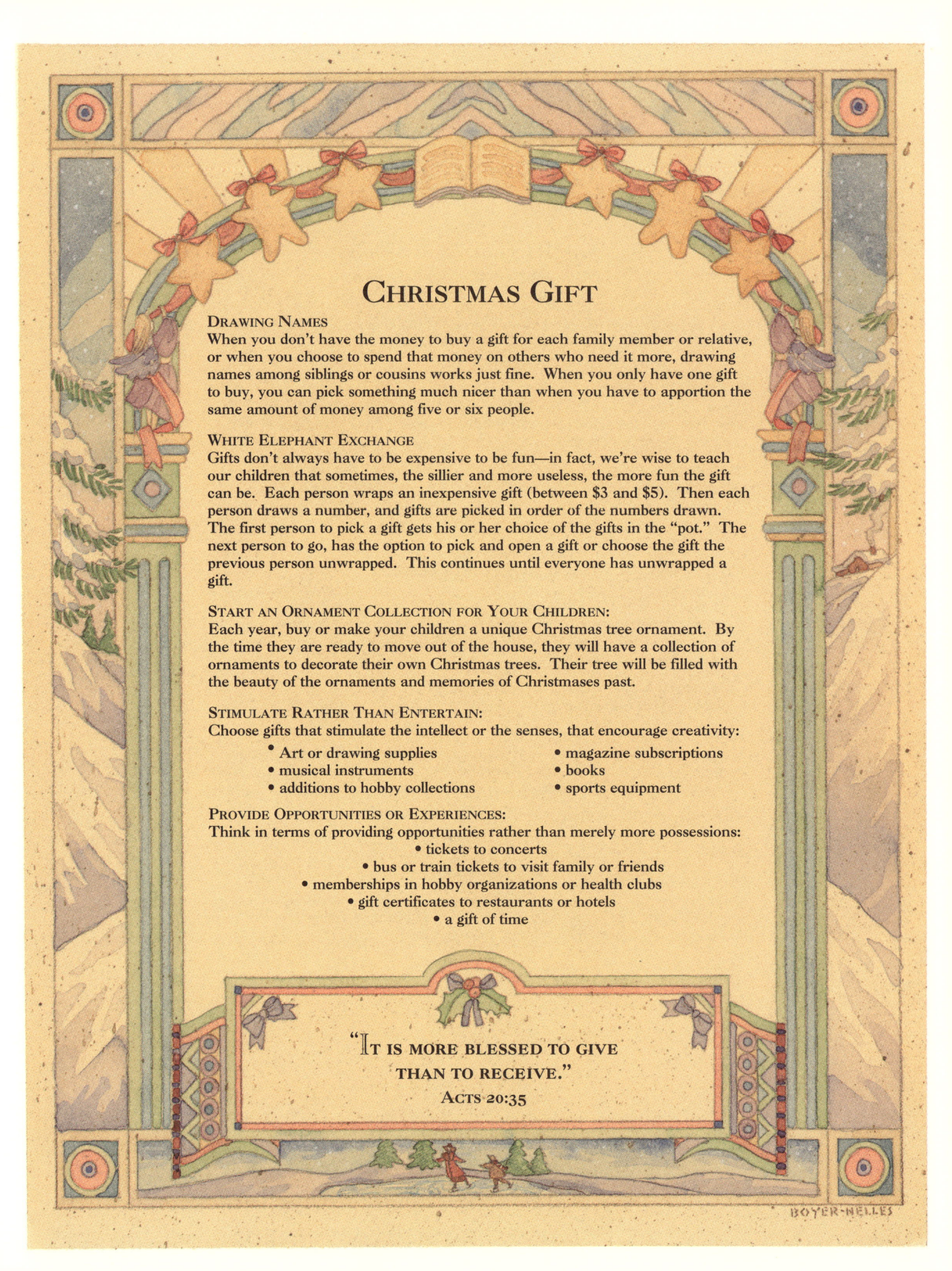

Drawing Names
When you don't have the money to buy a gift for each family member or relative, or when you choose to spend that money on others who need it more, drawing names among siblings or cousins works just fine. When you only have one gift to buy, you can pick something much nicer than when you have to apportion the same amount of money among five or six people.

White Elephant Exchange
Gifts don't always have to be expensive to be fun—in fact, we're wise to teach our children that sometimes, the sillier and more useless, the more fun the gift can be. Each person wraps an inexpensive gift (between $3 and $5). Then each person draws a number, and gifts are picked in order of the numbers drawn. The first person to pick a gift gets his or her choice of the gifts in the "pot." The next person to go, has the option to pick and open a gift or choose the gift the previous person unwrapped. This continues until everyone has unwrapped a gift.

Start an Ornament Collection for Your Children:
Each year, buy or make your children a unique Christmas tree ornament. By the time they are ready to move out of the house, they will have a collection of ornaments to decorate their own Christmas trees. Their tree will be filled with the beauty of the ornaments and memories of Christmases past.

Stimulate Rather Than Entertain:
Choose gifts that stimulate the intellect or the senses, that encourage creativity:

- Art or drawing supplies
- musical instruments
- additions to hobby collections
- magazine subscriptions
- books
- sports equipment

Provide Opportunities or Experiences:
Think in terms of providing opportunities rather than merely more possessions:

- tickets to concerts
- bus or train tickets to visit family or friends
- memberships in hobby organizations or health clubs
- gift certificates to restaurants or hotels
- a gift of time

> "It is more blessed to give than to receive."
> Acts 20:35

CHRISTMAS GIFTS

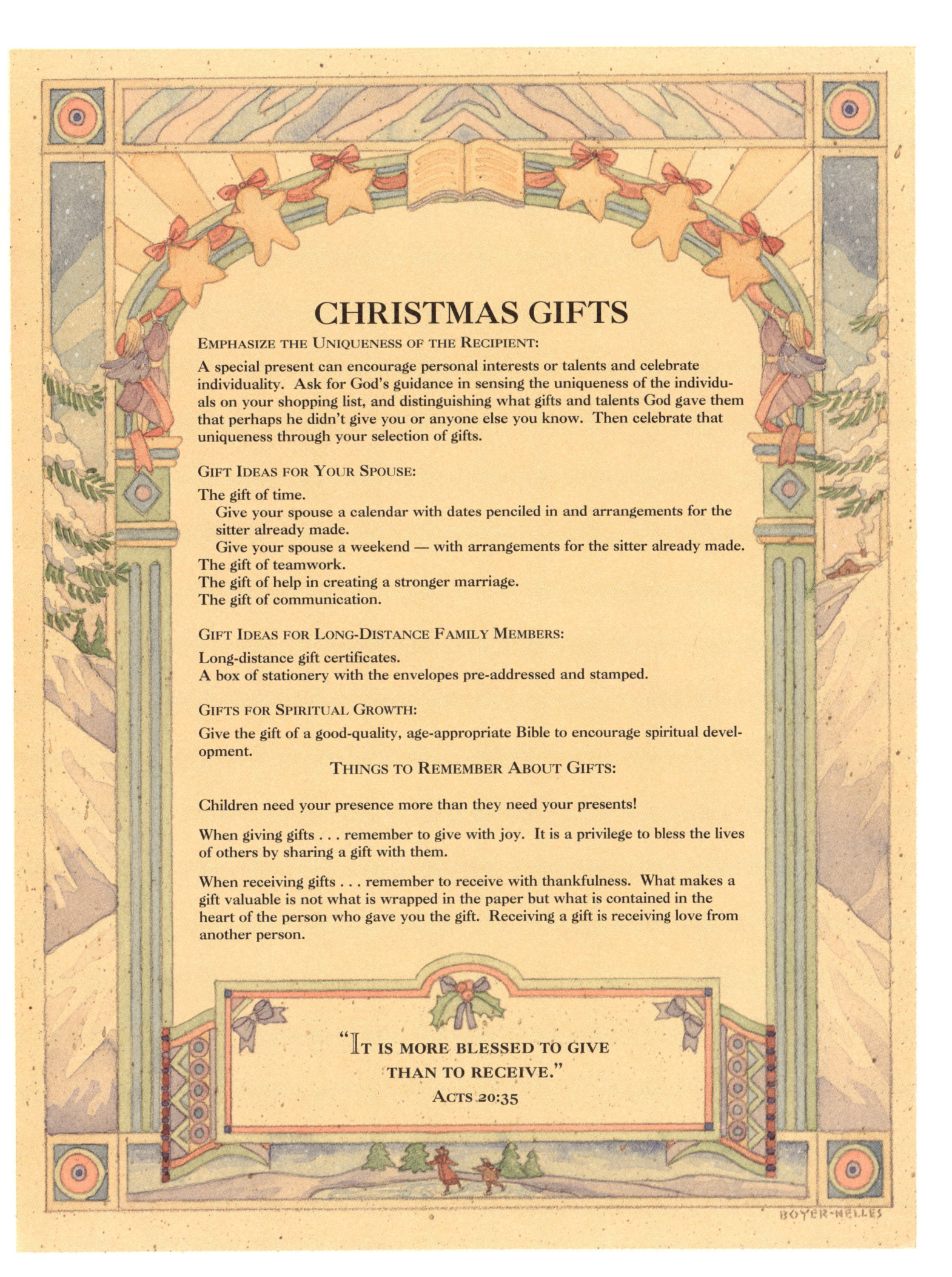

EMPHASIZE THE UNIQUENESS OF THE RECIPIENT:

A special present can encourage personal interests or talents and celebrate individuality. Ask for God's guidance in sensing the uniqueness of the individuals on your shopping list, and distinguishing what gifts and talents God gave them that perhaps he didn't give you or anyone else you know. Then celebrate that uniqueness through your selection of gifts.

GIFT IDEAS FOR YOUR SPOUSE:

The gift of time.
    Give your spouse a calendar with dates penciled in and arrangements for the sitter already made.
    Give your spouse a weekend — with arrangements for the sitter already made.
The gift of teamwork.
The gift of help in creating a stronger marriage.
The gift of communication.

GIFT IDEAS FOR LONG-DISTANCE FAMILY MEMBERS:

Long-distance gift certificates.
A box of stationery with the envelopes pre-addressed and stamped.

GIFTS FOR SPIRITUAL GROWTH:

Give the gift of a good-quality, age-appropriate Bible to encourage spiritual development.

THINGS TO REMEMBER ABOUT GIFTS:

Children need your presence more than they need your presents!

When giving gifts . . . remember to give with joy. It is a privilege to bless the lives of others by sharing a gift with them.

When receiving gifts . . . remember to receive with thankfulness. What makes a gift valuable is not what is wrapped in the paper but what is contained in the heart of the person who gave you the gift. Receiving a gift is receiving love from another person.

> "IT IS MORE BLESSED TO GIVE THAN TO RECEIVE."
> ACTS 20:35

Christmas Gift List

Use this list to track the special people in your life and their special interests. Celebrate their uniqueness through your selection of gifts.

PERSON	INTERESTS

"It is more blessed to give than to receive."
Acts 20:35

Christmas Gift List

PERSON   INTERESTS

_____   _____
_____   _____
_____   _____
_____   _____
_____   _____
_____   _____
_____   _____
_____   _____
_____   _____

"It is more blessed to give than to receive."
Acts 20:35

"In the beginning was the word,
and the word was with God,
and the word was God."
John 1:1

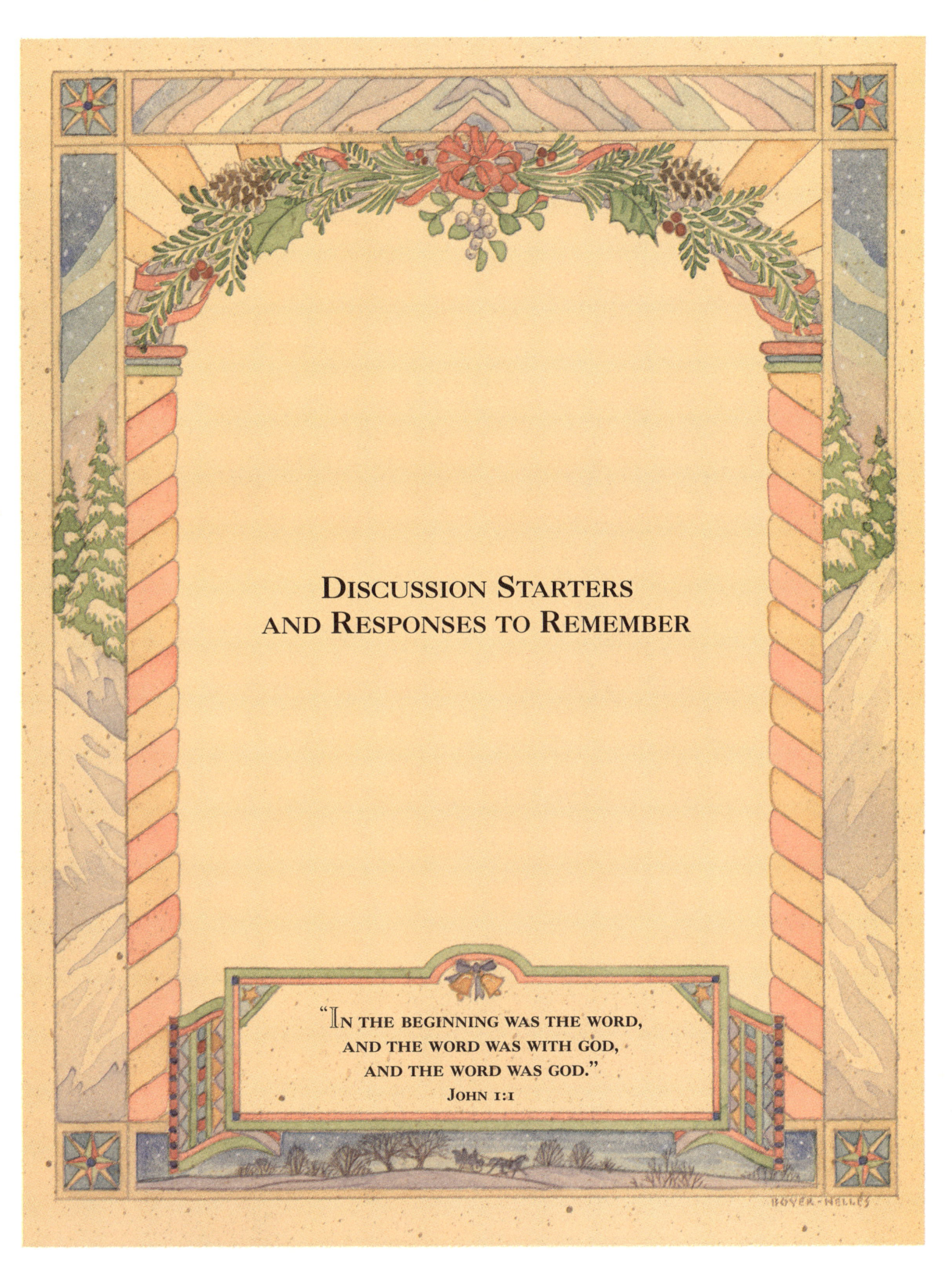

Discussion Starters
and Responses to Remember

"In the beginning was the Word,
and the Word was with God,
and the Word was God."
John 1:1

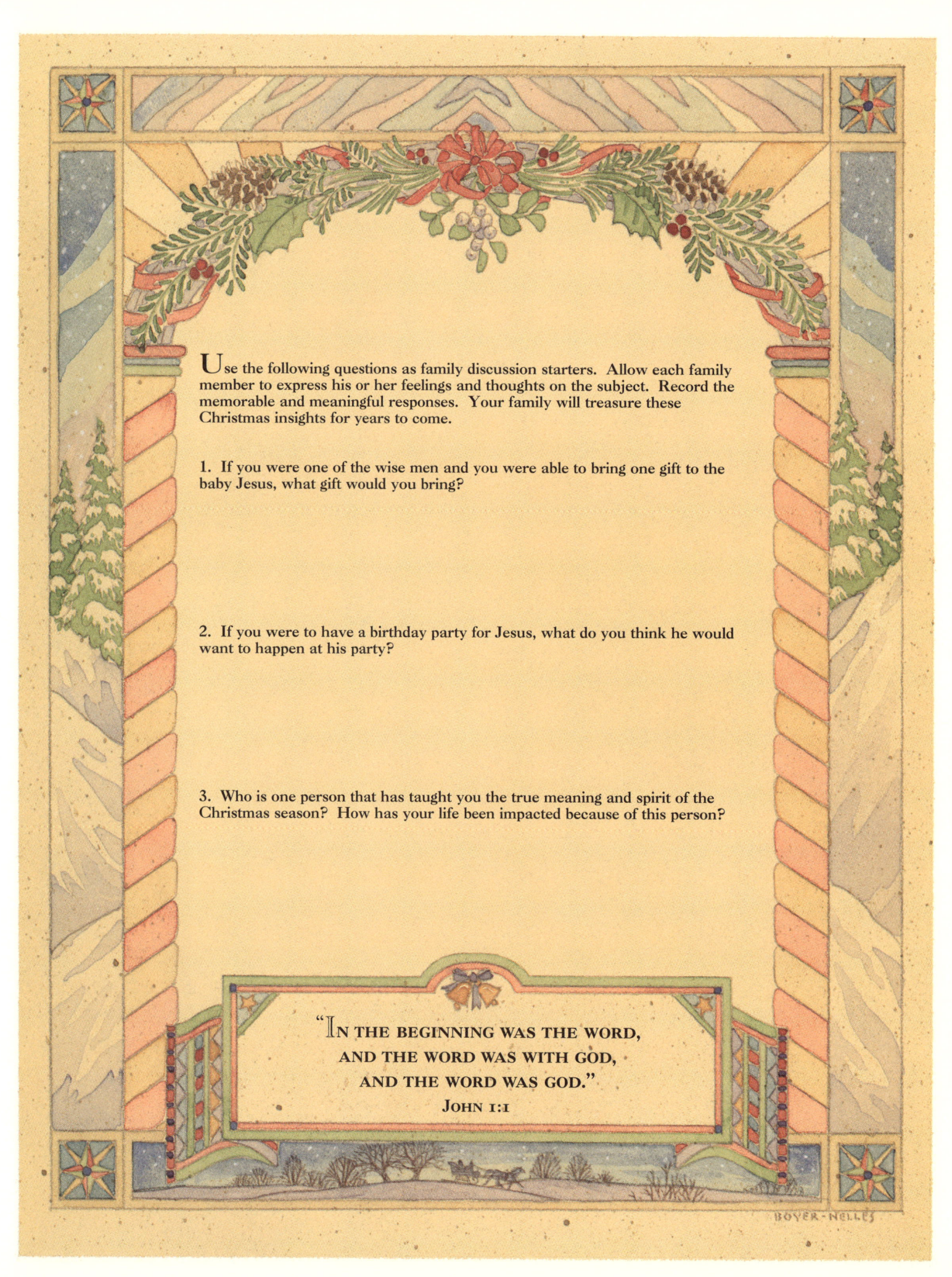

Use the following questions as family discussion starters. Allow each family member to express his or her feelings and thoughts on the subject. Record the memorable and meaningful responses. Your family will treasure these Christmas insights for years to come.

1. If you were one of the wise men and you were able to bring one gift to the baby Jesus, what gift would you bring?

2. If you were to have a birthday party for Jesus, what do you think he would want to happen at his party?

3. Who is one person that has taught you the true meaning and spirit of the Christmas season? How has your life been impacted because of this person?

"IN THE BEGINNING WAS THE WORD,
AND THE WORD WAS WITH GOD,
AND THE WORD WAS GOD."
JOHN 1:1

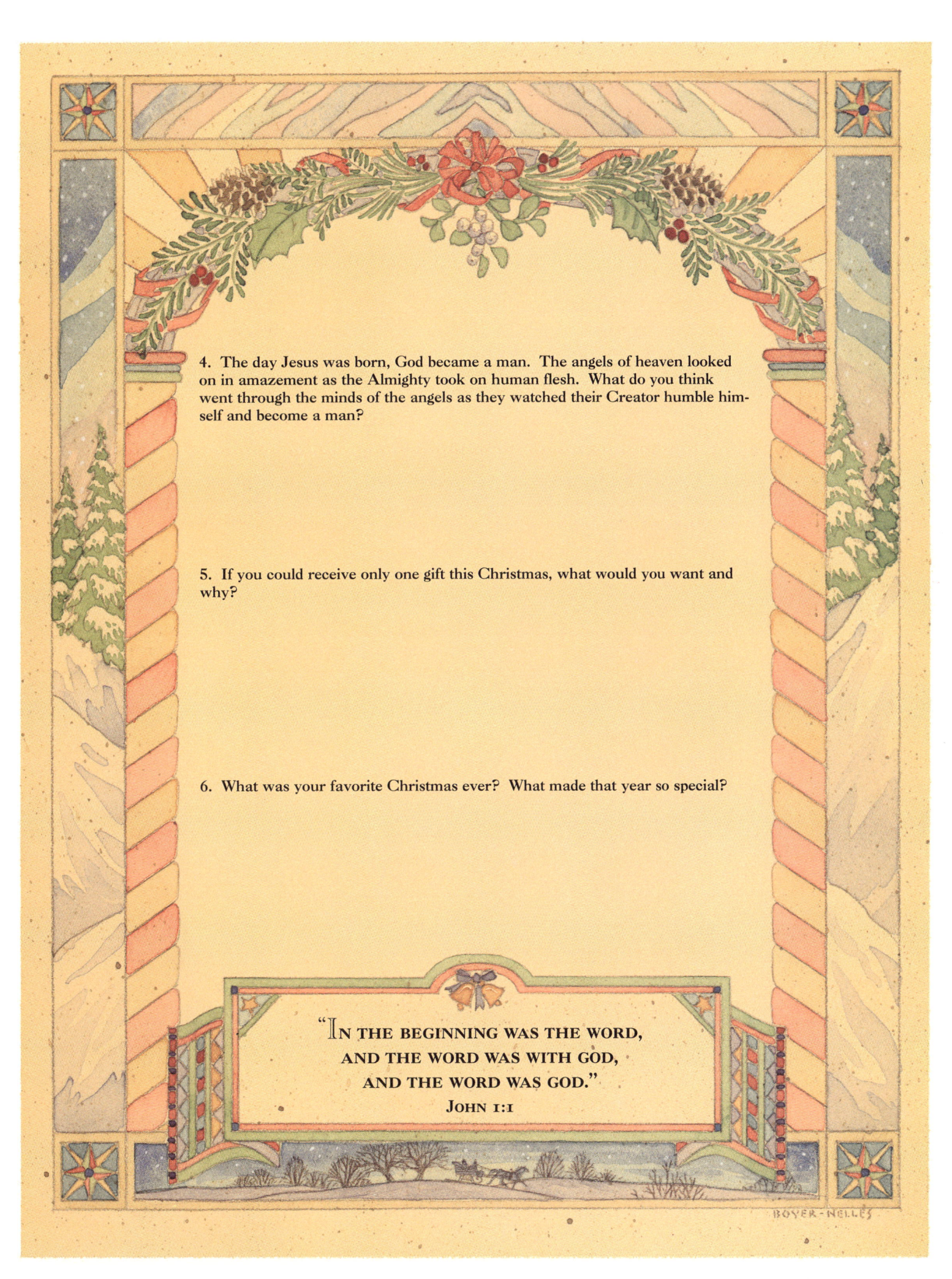

4. The day Jesus was born, God became a man. The angels of heaven looked on in amazement as the Almighty took on human flesh. What do you think went through the minds of the angels as they watched their Creator humble himself and become a man?

5. If you could receive only one gift this Christmas, what would you want and why?

6. What was your favorite Christmas ever? What made that year so special?

"IN THE BEGINNING WAS THE WORD,
AND THE WORD WAS WITH GOD,
AND THE WORD WAS GOD."

JOHN 1:1

"THE TRUE LIGHT THAT GIVES LIGHT TO EVERY MAN WAS COMING INTO THE WORLD."
JOHN 1:9

Make the Season Bright

"The true light that gives light to every man was coming into the world."
John 1:9

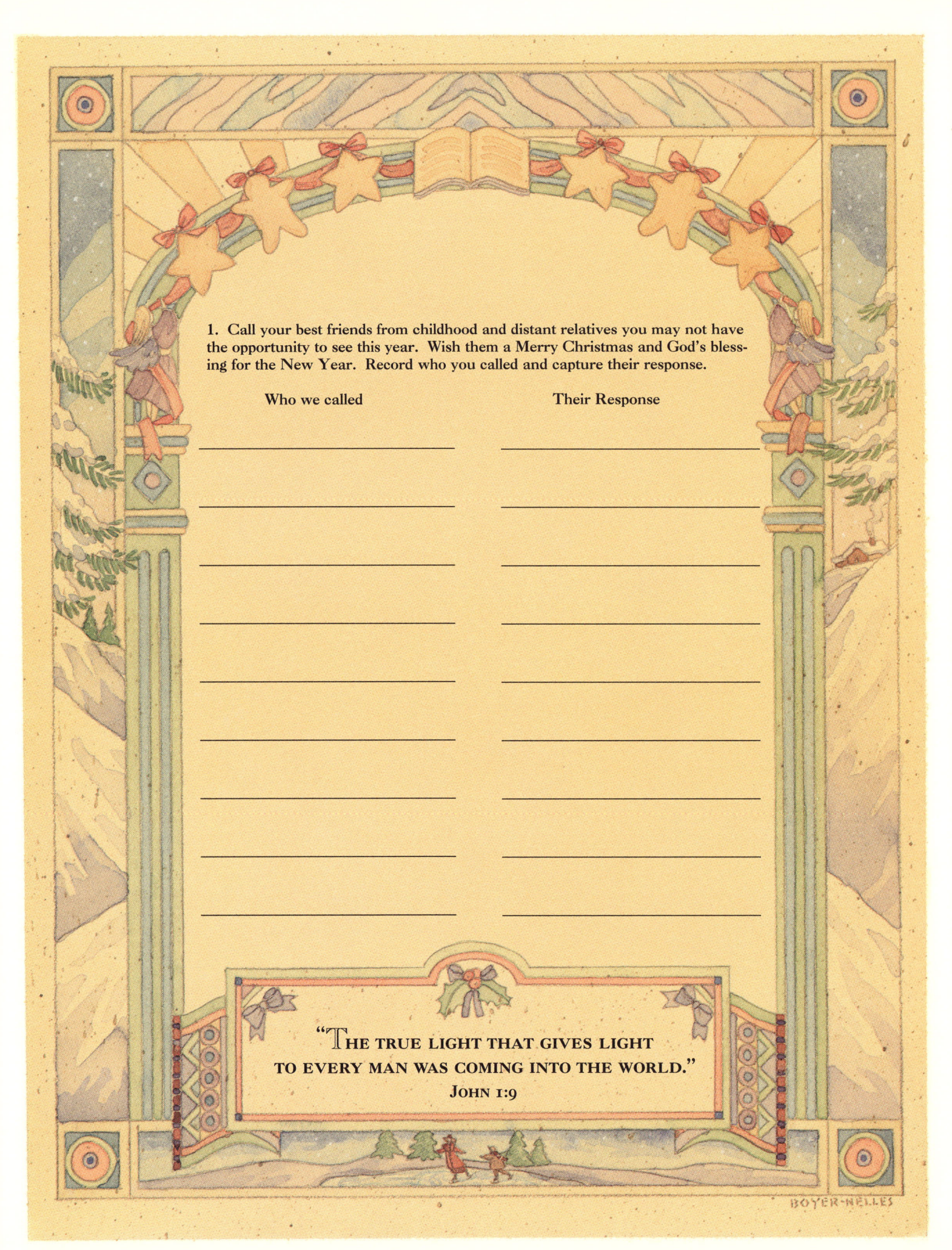

1. Call your best friends from childhood and distant relatives you may not have the opportunity to see this year. Wish them a Merry Christmas and God's blessing for the New Year. Record who you called and capture their response.

Who we called	Their Response
_____	_____
_____	_____
_____	_____
_____	_____
_____	_____
_____	_____
_____	_____
_____	_____

"THE TRUE LIGHT THAT GIVES LIGHT TO EVERY MAN WAS COMING INTO THE WORLD."
JOHN 1:9

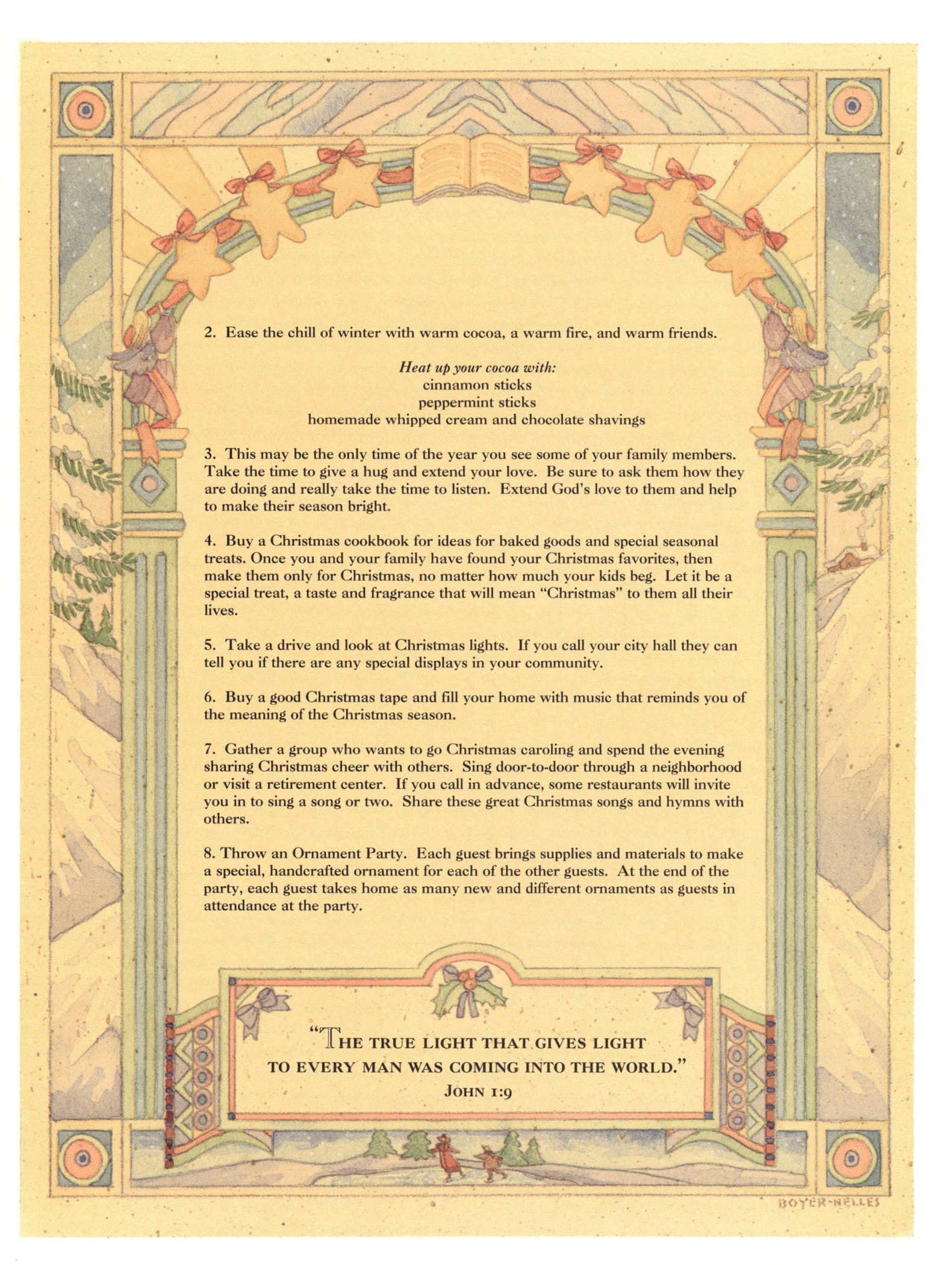

2. Ease the chill of winter with warm cocoa, a warm fire, and warm friends.

Heat up your cocoa with:
cinnamon sticks
peppermint sticks
homemade whipped cream and chocolate shavings

3. This may be the only time of the year you see some of your family members. Take the time to give a hug and extend your love. Be sure to ask them how they are doing and really take the time to listen. Extend God's love to them and help to make their season bright.

4. Buy a Christmas cookbook for ideas for baked goods and special seasonal treats. Once you and your family have found your Christmas favorites, then make them only for Christmas, no matter how much your kids beg. Let it be a special treat, a taste and fragrance that will mean "Christmas" to them all their lives.

5. Take a drive and look at Christmas lights. If you call your city hall they can tell you if there are any special displays in your community.

6. Buy a good Christmas tape and fill your home with music that reminds you of the meaning of the Christmas season.

7. Gather a group who wants to go Christmas caroling and spend the evening sharing Christmas cheer with others. Sing door-to-door through a neighborhood or visit a retirement center. If you call in advance, some restaurants will invite you in to sing a song or two. Share these great Christmas songs and hymns with others.

8. Throw an Ornament Party. Each guest brings supplies and materials to make a special, handcrafted ornament for each of the other guests. At the end of the party, each guest takes home as many new and different ornaments as guests in attendance at the party.

"THE TRUE LIGHT THAT GIVES LIGHT
TO EVERY MAN WAS COMING INTO THE WORLD."
JOHN 1:9

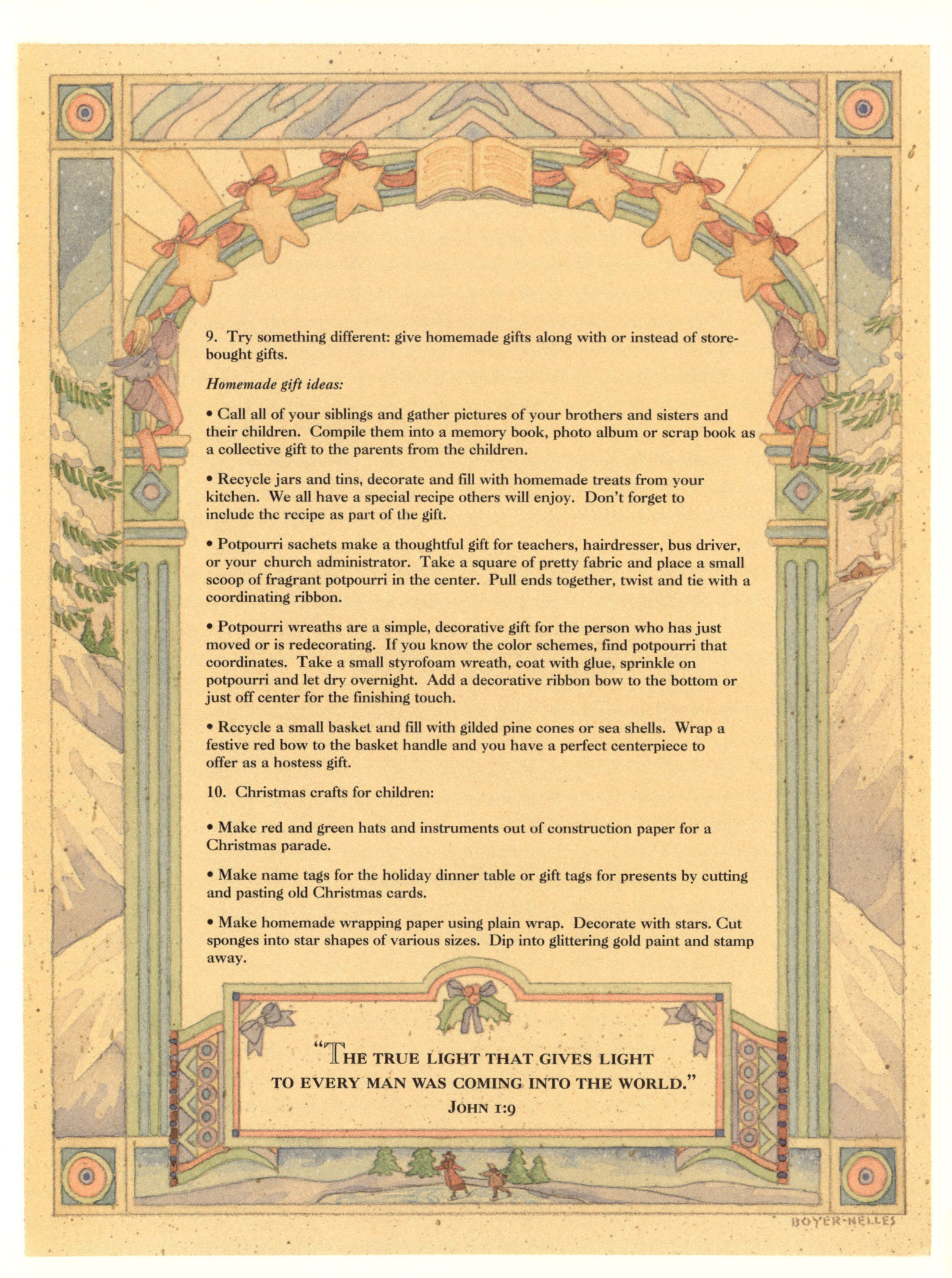

9. Try something different: give homemade gifts along with or instead of store-bought gifts.

Homemade gift ideas:

• Call all of your siblings and gather pictures of your brothers and sisters and their children. Compile them into a memory book, photo album or scrap book as a collective gift to the parents from the children.

• Recycle jars and tins, decorate and fill with homemade treats from your kitchen. We all have a special recipe others will enjoy. Don't forget to include the recipe as part of the gift.

• Potpourri sachets make a thoughtful gift for teachers, hairdresser, bus driver, or your church administrator. Take a square of pretty fabric and place a small scoop of fragrant potpourri in the center. Pull ends together, twist and tie with a coordinating ribbon.

• Potpourri wreaths are a simple, decorative gift for the person who has just moved or is redecorating. If you know the color schemes, find potpourri that coordinates. Take a small styrofoam wreath, coat with glue, sprinkle on potpourri and let dry overnight. Add a decorative ribbon bow to the bottom or just off center for the finishing touch.

• Recycle a small basket and fill with gilded pine cones or sea shells. Wrap a festive red bow to the basket handle and you have a perfect centerpiece to offer as a hostess gift.

10. Christmas crafts for children:

• Make red and green hats and instruments out of construction paper for a Christmas parade.

• Make name tags for the holiday dinner table or gift tags for presents by cutting and pasting old Christmas cards.

• Make homemade wrapping paper using plain wrap. Decorate with stars. Cut sponges into star shapes of various sizes. Dip into glittering gold paint and stamp away.

"The true light that gives light to every man was coming into the world."
John 1:9

11. Celebrate the "Reason for the Season" with friends and family members by reading the Christmas story from Luke 2:1-20 and Matthew 2:1-12. Share what this story means to you.

Reflections:

"THE TRUE LIGHT THAT GIVES LIGHT
TO EVERY MAN WAS COMING INTO THE WORLD."
JOHN 1:9

12. Invite friends over for hot cider and donuts.

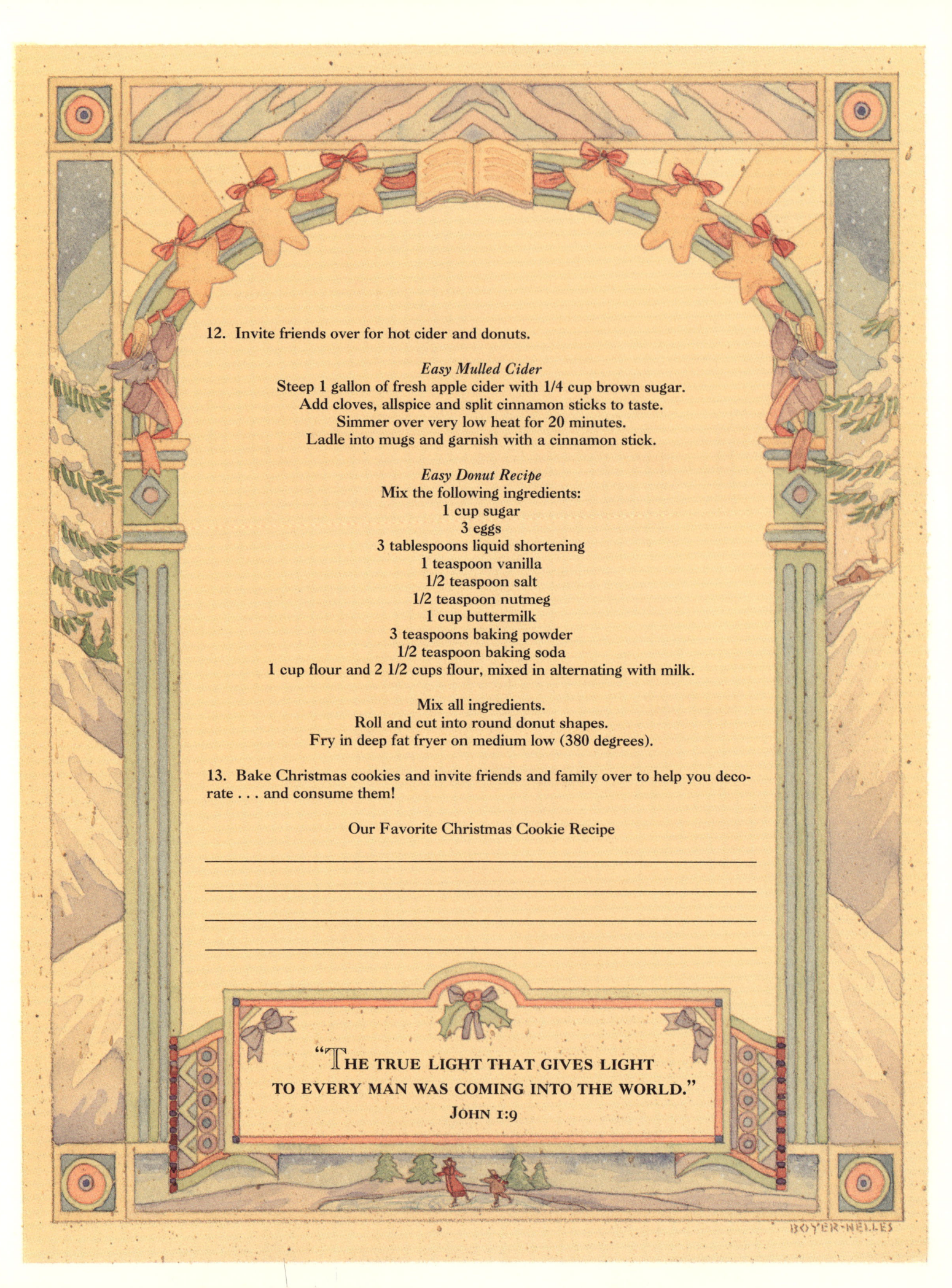

Easy Mulled Cider
Steep 1 gallon of fresh apple cider with 1/4 cup brown sugar.
Add cloves, allspice and split cinnamon sticks to taste.
Simmer over very low heat for 20 minutes.
Ladle into mugs and garnish with a cinnamon stick.

Easy Donut Recipe
Mix the following ingredients:
1 cup sugar
3 eggs
3 tablespoons liquid shortening
1 teaspoon vanilla
1/2 teaspoon salt
1/2 teaspoon nutmeg
1 cup buttermilk
3 teaspoons baking powder
1/2 teaspoon baking soda
1 cup flour and 2 1/2 cups flour, mixed in alternating with milk.

Mix all ingredients.
Roll and cut into round donut shapes.
Fry in deep fat fryer on medium low (380 degrees).

13. Bake Christmas cookies and invite friends and family over to help you decorate . . . and consume them!

Our Favorite Christmas Cookie Recipe

_____
_____
_____
_____

"THE TRUE LIGHT THAT GIVES LIGHT
TO EVERY MAN WAS COMING INTO THE WORLD."
JOHN 1:9

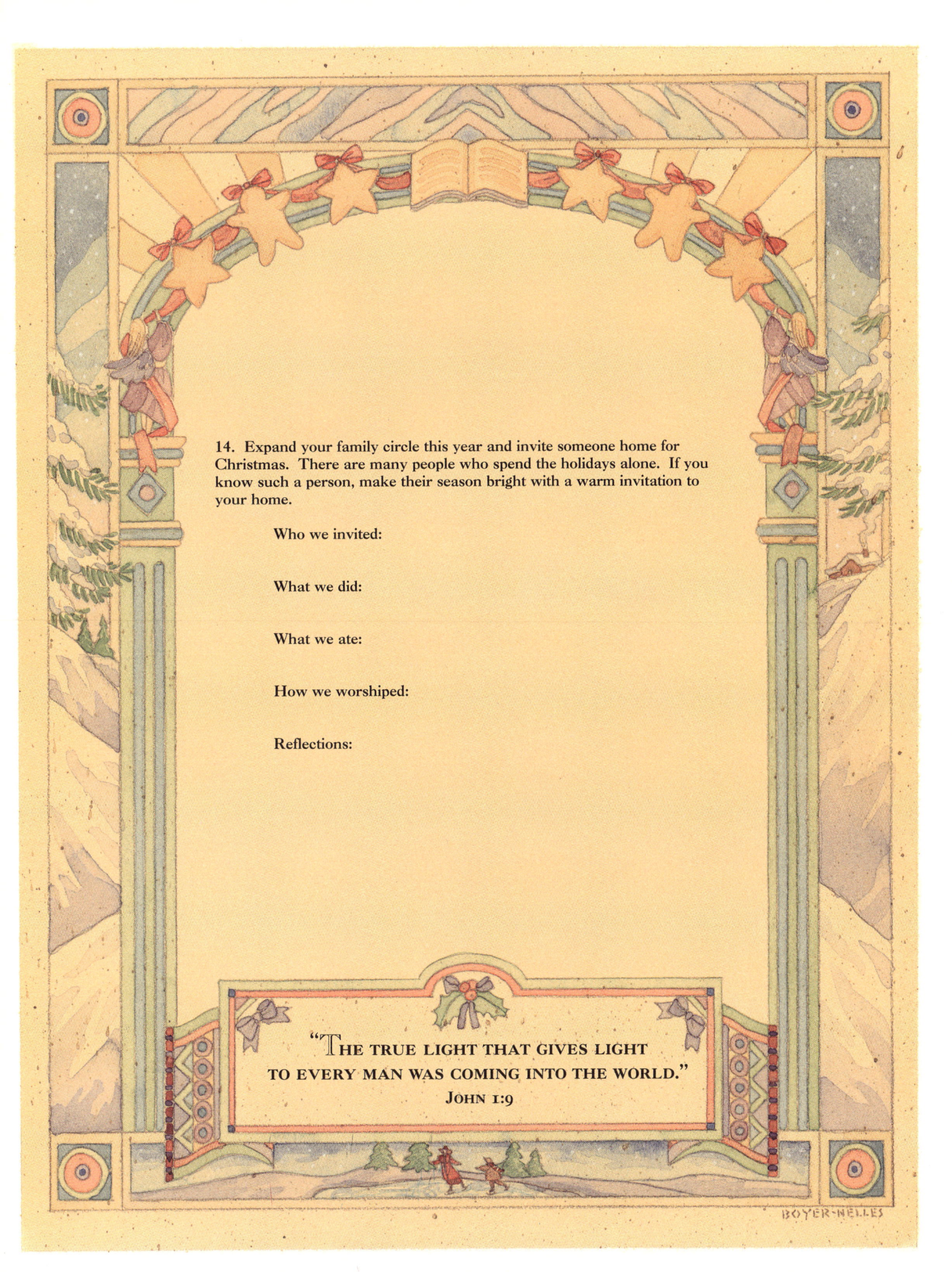

14. Expand your family circle this year and invite someone home for Christmas. There are many people who spend the holidays alone. If you know such a person, make their season bright with a warm invitation to your home.

    Who we invited:

    What we did:

    What we ate:

    How we worshiped:

    Reflections:

"THE TRUE LIGHT THAT GIVES LIGHT TO EVERY MAN WAS COMING INTO THE WORLD."
JOHN 1:9

"For where your treasure is, there your heart will be also."
Matthew 6:21

Christmas Memories to Treasure

"For where your treasure is, there your heart will be also."
Matthew 6:21

CHRISTMAS MOMENTS

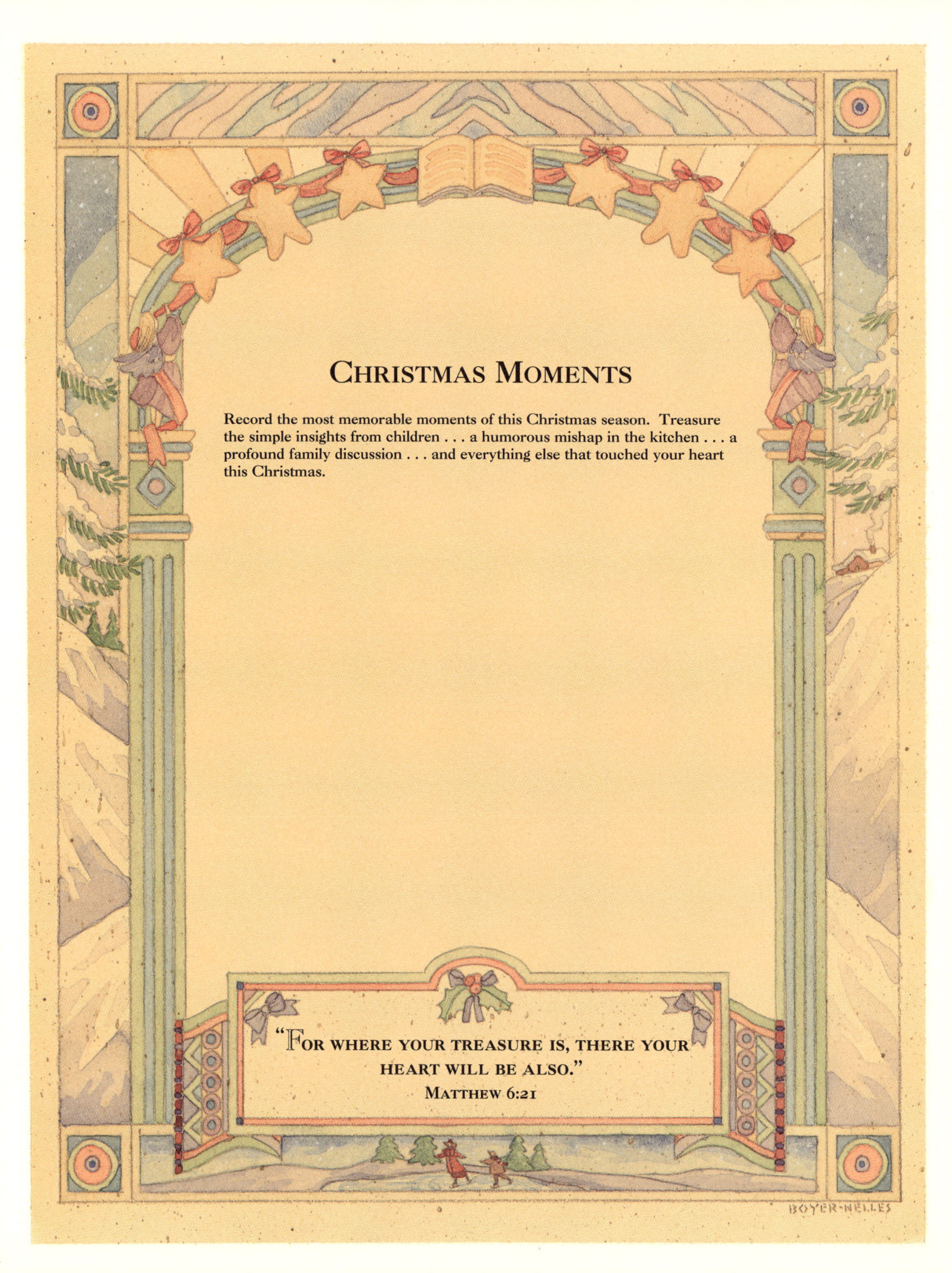

Record the most memorable moments of this Christmas season. Treasure the simple insights from children . . . a humorous mishap in the kitchen . . . a profound family discussion . . . and everything else that touched your heart this Christmas.

"FOR WHERE YOUR TREASURE IS, THERE YOUR HEART WILL BE ALSO."
MATTHEW 6:21

CHRISTMAS PRAYERS

Write your own Family Christmas Prayer. Let each family member contribute his or her words and thoughts. Compile and record the prayer here and make it a treasured part of your Christmas tradition.

"For where your treasure is, there you heart will be also."

Matthew 6:21

Christmas Gatherings

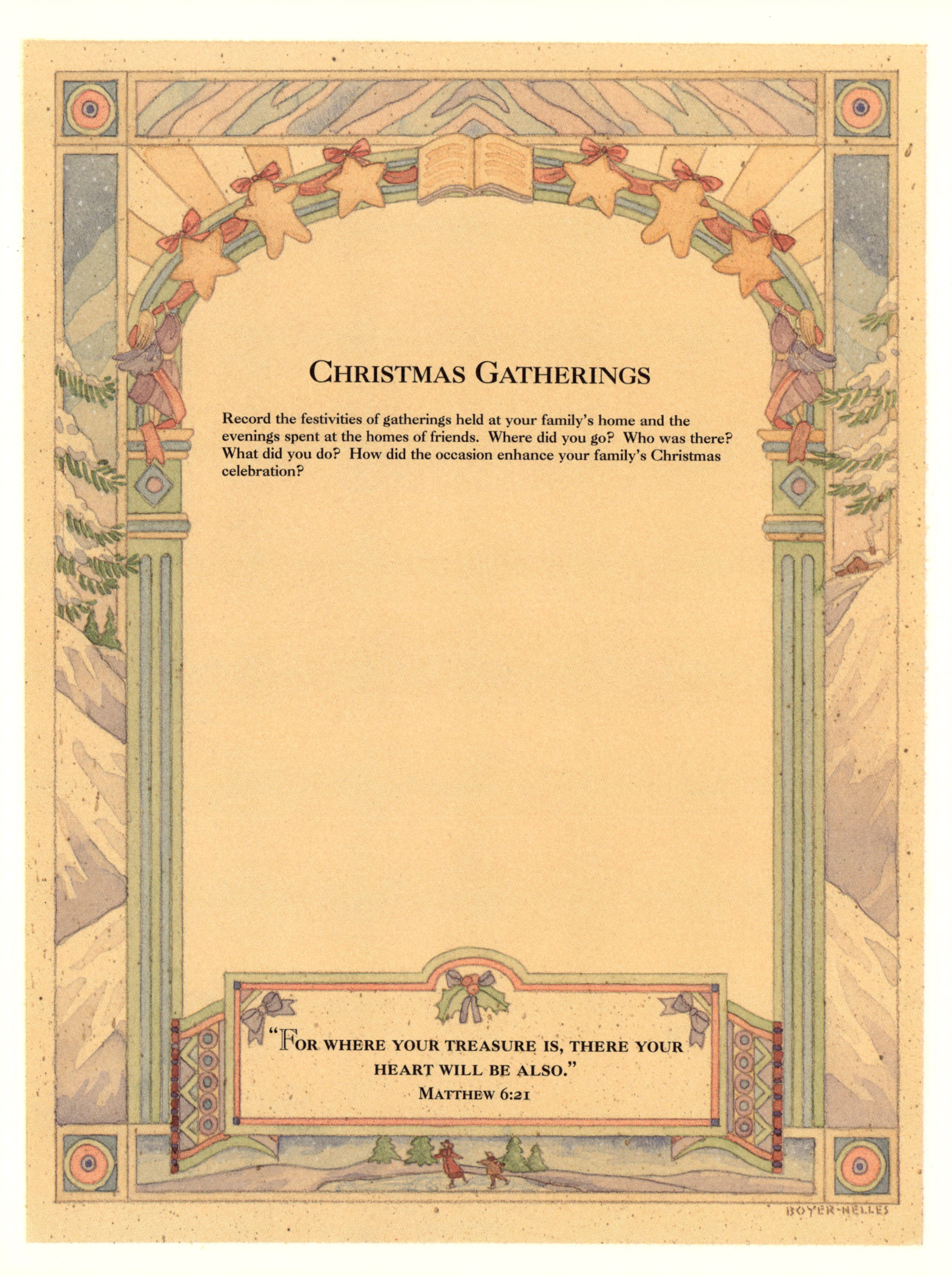

Record the festivities of gatherings held at your family's home and the evenings spent at the homes of friends. Where did you go? Who was there? What did you do? How did the occasion enhance your family's Christmas celebration?

"For where your treasure is, there your heart will be also."
Matthew 6:21

Christmas Worship

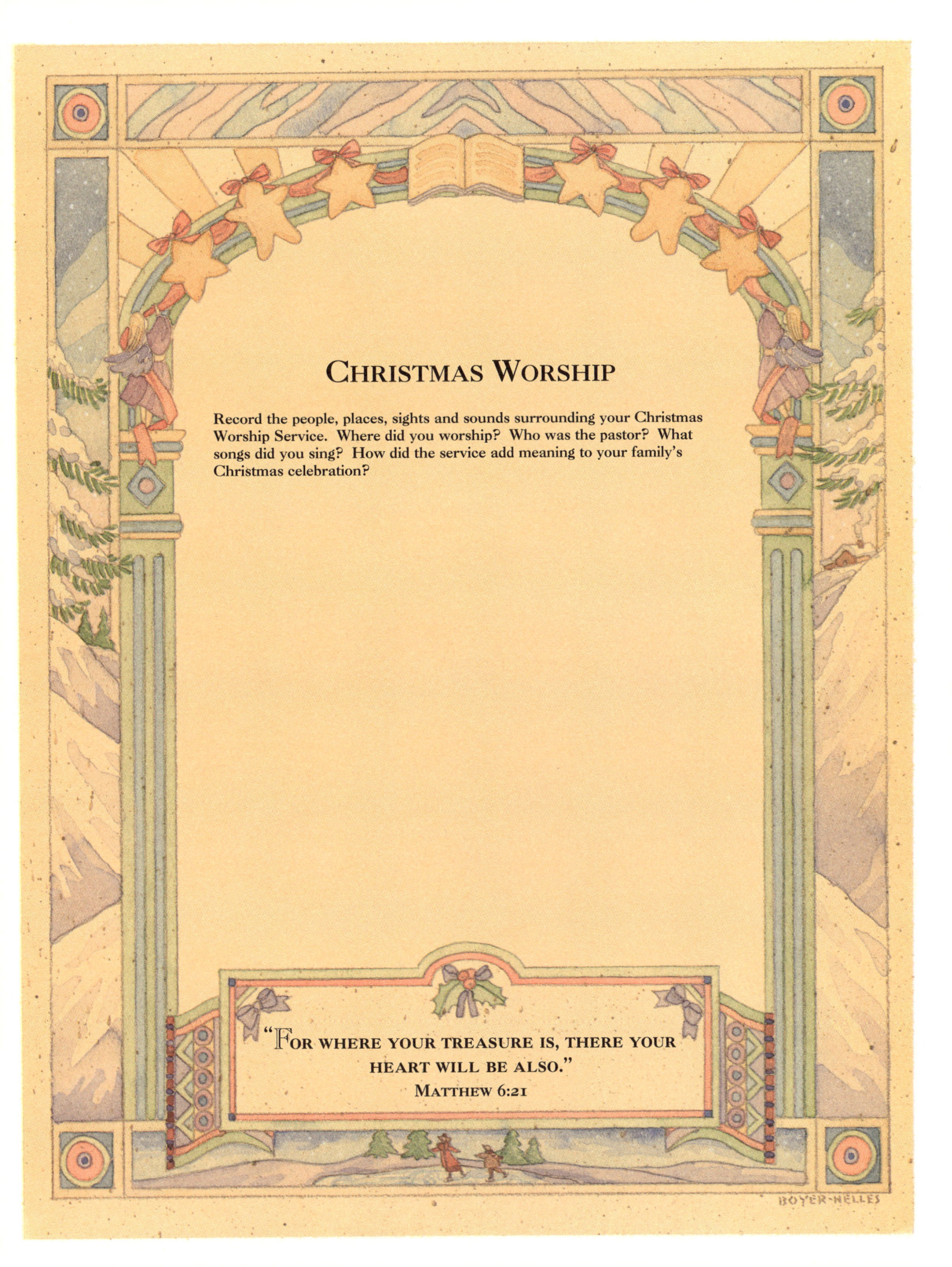

Record the people, places, sights and sounds surrounding your Christmas Worship Service. Where did you worship? Who was the pastor? What songs did you sing? How did the service add meaning to your family's Christmas celebration?

"For where your treasure is, there your heart will be also."
Matthew 6:21

"For I know the plans I have for you," declares the Lord, "plans to prosper you and not to harm you, plans to give you a hope and a future."
Jeremiah 29:11

Thoughts for the New Year

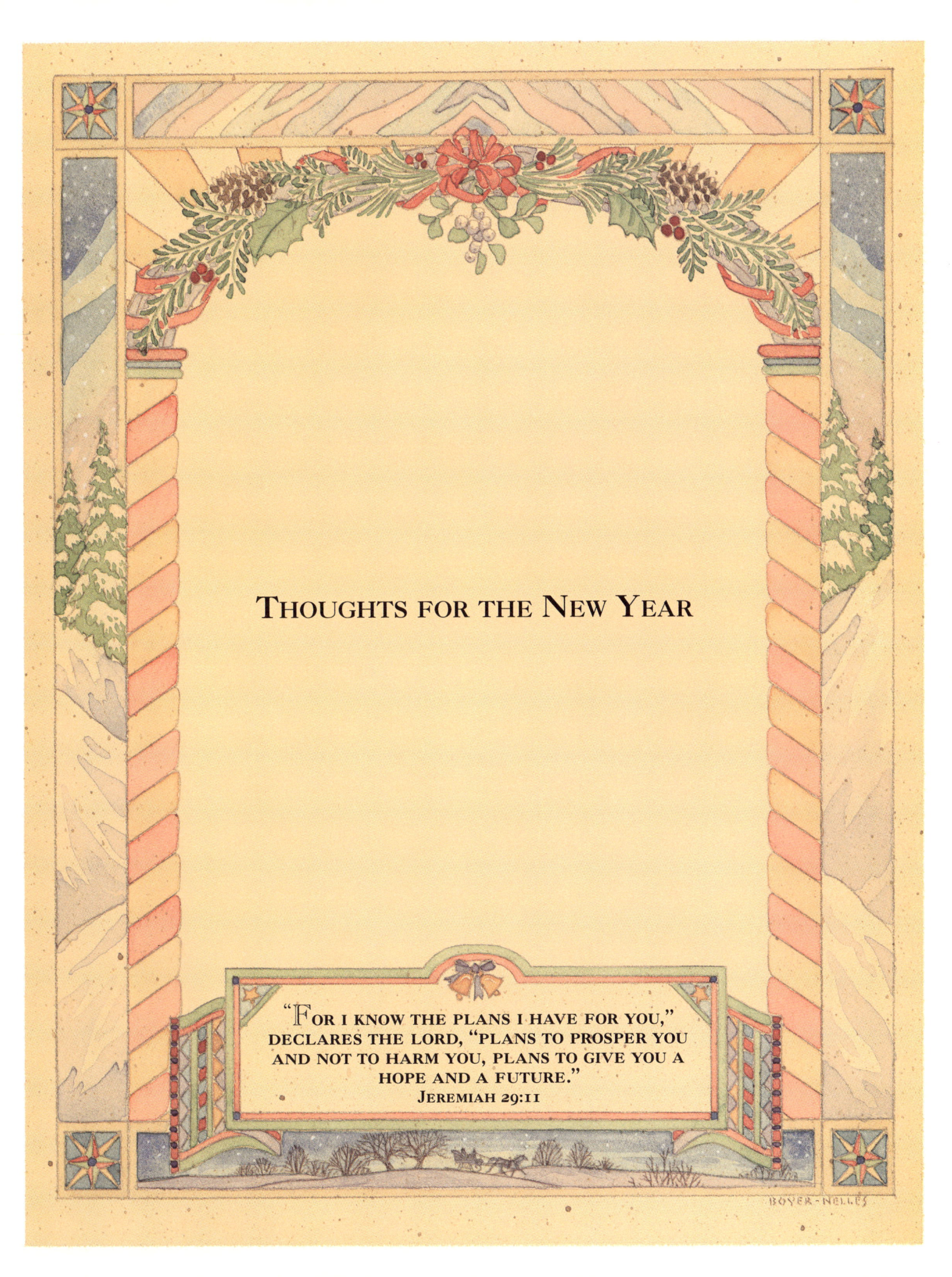

"For I know the plans I have for you," declares the Lord, "plans to prosper you and not to harm you, plans to give you a hope and a future."
Jeremiah 29:11

THOUGHTS FOR THE NEW YEAR

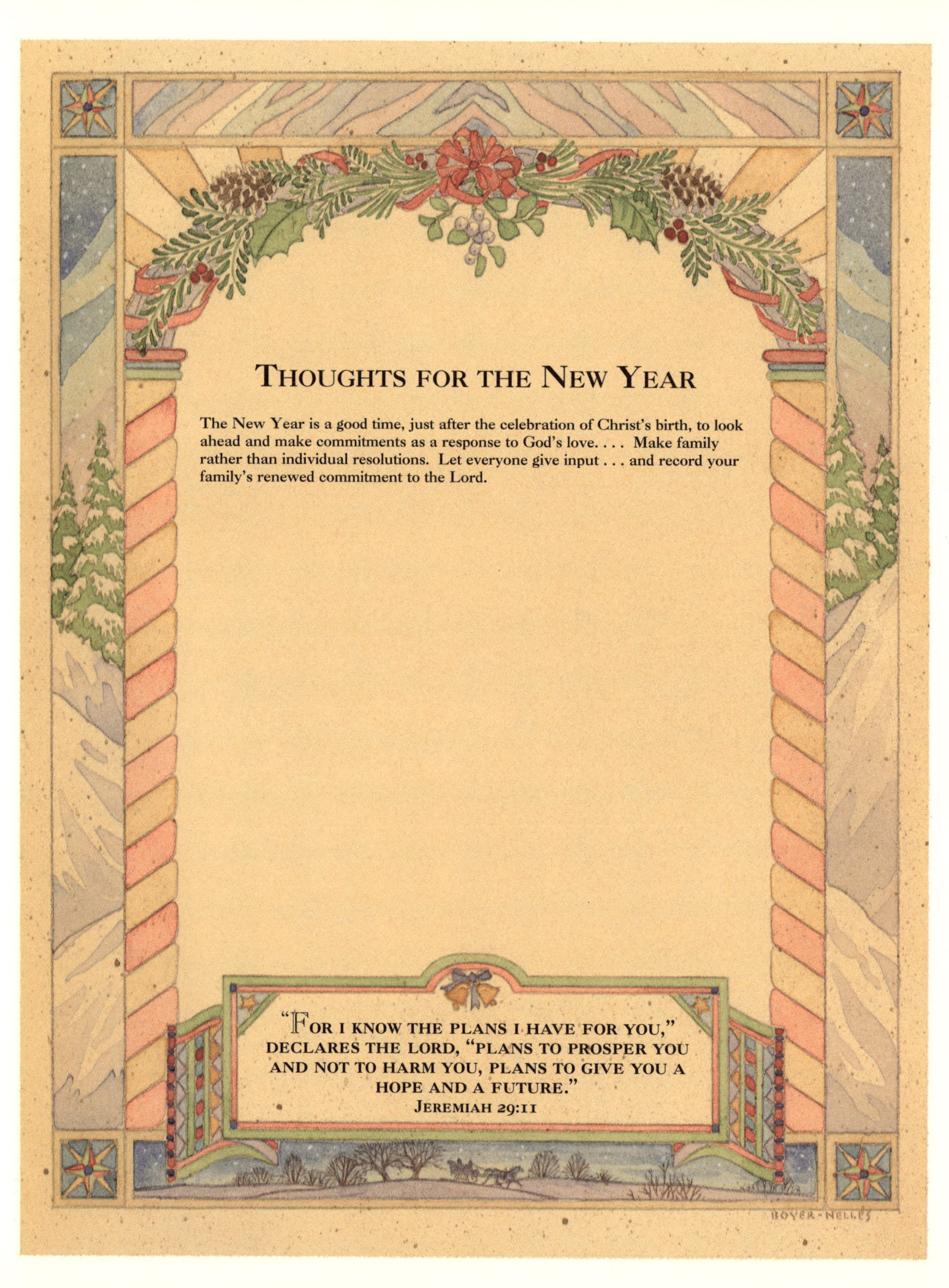

The New Year is a good time, just after the celebration of Christ's birth, to look ahead and make commitments as a response to God's love. . . . Make family rather than individual resolutions. Let everyone give input . . . and record your family's renewed commitment to the Lord.

"For I know the plans I have for you," declares the Lord, "plans to prosper you and not to harm you, plans to give you a hope and a future."
Jeremiah 29:11

Thoughts for the New Year

"For I know the plans I have for you," declares the Lord, "plans to prosper you and not to harm you, plans to give you a hope and a future."

Jeremiah 29:11

GOALS FOR THE NEW YEAR

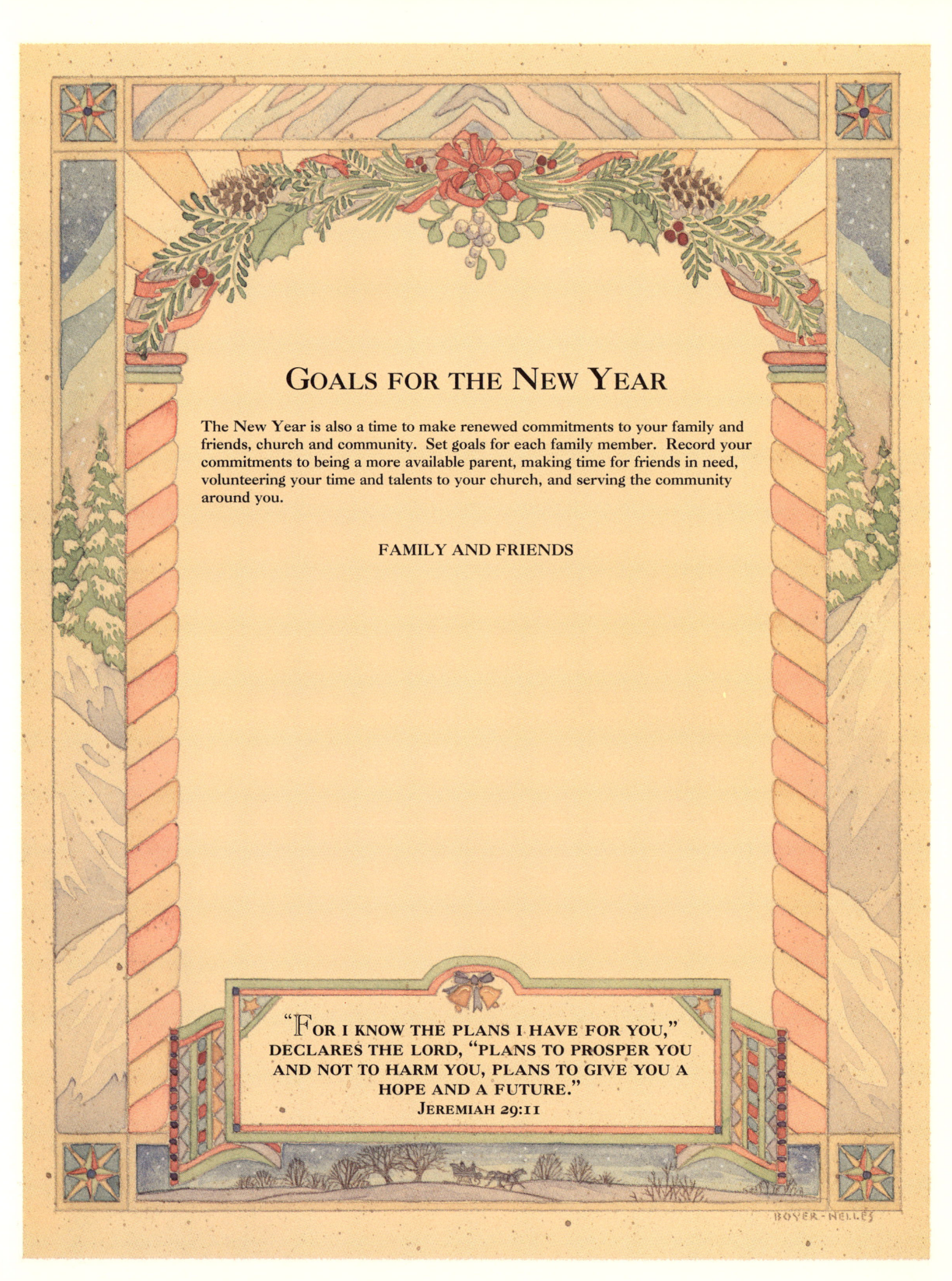

The New Year is also a time to make renewed commitments to your family and friends, church and community. Set goals for each family member. Record your commitments to being a more available parent, making time for friends in need, volunteering your time and talents to your church, and serving the community around you.

FAMILY AND FRIENDS

"For I know the plans I have for you," declares the Lord, "plans to prosper you and not to harm you, plans to give you a hope and a future."
Jeremiah 29:11

Goals for the New Year

Church and Community

"For I know the plans I have for you," declares the Lord, "plans to prosper you and not to harm you, plans to give you a hope and a future."
Jeremiah 29:11

Thoughts for Next Christmas

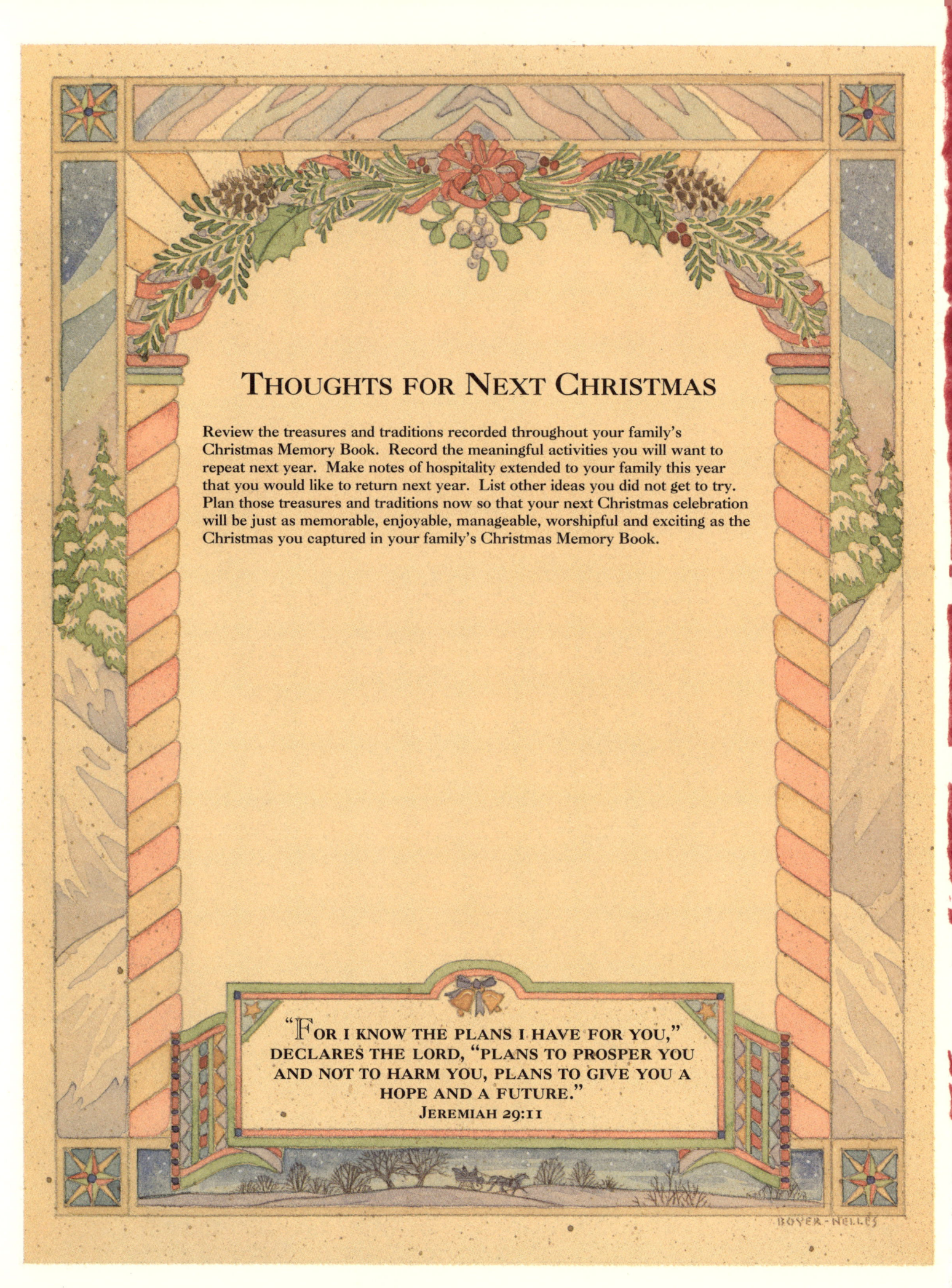

Review the treasures and traditions recorded throughout your family's Christmas Memory Book. Record the meaningful activities you will want to repeat next year. Make notes of hospitality extended to your family this year that you would like to return next year. List other ideas you did not get to try. Plan those treasures and traditions now so that your next Christmas celebration will be just as memorable, enjoyable, manageable, worshipful and exciting as the Christmas you captured in your family's Christmas Memory Book.

"For I know the plans I have for you," declares the Lord, "plans to prosper you and not to harm you, plans to give you a hope and a future."
Jeremiah 29:11